Chelsea

P9-DFQ-714

COMPREHENSIVE RESEARCH
AND STUDY GUIDE

BLOOM'S
MAJOR
DRAMATISTS

George Bernard Shaw

EDITED AND WITH AN
INTRODUCTION BY HAROLD BLOOM

CURRENTLY AVAILABLE

BLOOM'S MAJOR DRAMATISTS

Anton Chekhov
Henrik Ibsen
Arthur Miller
Eugene O'Neill
Shakespeare's Comedies
Shakespeare's Histories
Shakespeare's Romances
Shakespeare's Tragedies
George Bernard Shaw
Tennessee Williams

BLOOM'S MAJOR NOVELISTS

Jane Austen
The Brontës
Willa Cather
Charles Dickens
William Faulkner
F. Scott Fitzgerald
Nathaniel Hawthorne
Ernest Hemingway
Toni Morrison
John Steinbeck
Mark Twain
Alice Walker

BLOOM'S MAJOR SHORT STORY WRITERS

William Faulkner
F. Scott Fitzgerald
Ernest Hemingway
O. Henry
James Joyce
Herman Melville
Flannery O'Connor
Edgar Allan Poe
J. D. Salinger
John Steinbeck
Mark Twain
Eudora Welty

BLOOM'S MAJOR WORLD POETS

Geoffrey Chaucer
Emily Dickinson
John Donne
T. S. Eliot
Robert Frost
Langston Hughes
John Milton
Edgar Allan Poe
Shakespeare's Poems & Sonnets
Alfred, Lord Tennyson
Walt Whitman
William Wordsworth

BLOOM'S NOTES

The Adventures of Huckleberry Finn
Aeneid
The Age of Innocence
Animal Farm
The Autobiography of Malcolm X
The Awakening
Beloved
Beowulf
Billy Budd, Benito Cereno, & Bartleby the Scrivener
Brave New World
The Catcher in the Rye
Crime and Punishment
The Crucible

Death of a Salesman
A Farewell to Arms
Frankenstein
The Grapes of Wrath
Great Expectations
The Great Gatsby
Gulliver's Travels
Hamlet
Heart of Darkness & The Secret Sharer
Henry IV, Part One
I Know Why the Caged Bird Sings
Iliad
Inferno
Invisible Man
Jane Eyre
Julius Caesar

King Lear
Lord of the Flies
Macbeth
A Midsummer Night's Dream
Moby-Dick
Native Son
Nineteen Eighty-Four
Odyssey
Oedipus Plays
Of Mice and Men
The Old Man and the Sea
Othello
Paradise Lost
The Portrait of a Lady
A Portrait of the Artist as a Young Man

Pride and Prejudice
The Red Badge of Courage
Romeo and Juliet
The Scarlet Letter
Silas Marner
The Sound and the Fury
The Sun Also Rises
A Tale of Two Cities
Tess of the D'Urbervilles
Their Eyes Were Watching God
To Kill a Mockingbird
Uncle Tom's Cabin
Wuthering Heights

COMPREHENSIVE RESEARCH
AND STUDY GUIDE

BLOOM'S
MAJOR
DRAMATISTS

George Bernard Shaw

EDITED AND WITH AN INTRODUCTION
BY HAROLD BLOOM

© 2000 by Chelsea House Publishers, a division of Main Line Book Co.

Introduction © 2000 by Harold Bloom

Printed and bound in the United States of America.

First Printing
1 3 5 7 9 8 6 4 2

Library of Congress Cataloging-in-Publication Data
George Bernard Shaw / edited and with an introduction by Harold Bloom.
     p.   cm. — (Bloom's major dramatists)
   Includes bibliographical references and index.
   Summary: A comprehensive research and study guide for several
plays by George Bernard Shaw, including plot summaries, lists of
characters, and critical views.
    ISBN 0–7910–5237–0
    1. Shaw, Bernard, 1856–1950—Examinations Study guides.
[1. Shaw, Bernard, 1856–1950—Criticism and interpretation
2. English literature—History and criticism.]   I. Bloom, Harold.
II. Series.
PR5367.G43   1999
822.3'3—dc21   99–27601
                                              CIP

Chelsea House Publishers
1974 Sproul Road, Suite 400
Broomall, PA 19008-0914

The Chelsea House World Wide Web address is
http://www.chelseahouse.com

Contributing Editor: Elizabeth Beaudin

Contents

User's Guide

This volume is designed to present biographical, critical, and bibliographical information on the playwright's best-known or most important works. Following Harold Bloom's editor's note and introduction are a detailed biography of the author, discussing major life events and important literary accomplishments. A plot summary of each play follows, tracing significant themes, patterns, and motifs in the work.

A selection of critical extracts, derived from previously published material from leading critics, analyzes aspects of each play. The extracts consist of statements from the author, if available, early reviews of the work, and later evaluations up to the present. A bibliography of the author's writings (including a complete list of all works written, cowritten, edited, and translated), a list of additional books and articles on the author and his or her work, and an index of themes and ideas in the author's writings conclude the volume.

~

Harold Bloom is Sterling Professor of the Humanities at Yale University and Henry W. and Albert A. Berg Professor of English at the New York University Graduate School. He is the author of over 20 books and the editor of more than 30 anthologies of literary criticism.

Professor Bloom's works include *Shelley's Mythmaking* (1959), *The Visionary Company* (1961), *Blake's Apocalypse* (1963), *Yeats* (1970), *A Map of Misreading* (1975), *Kabbalah and Criticism* (1975), and *Agon: Toward a Theory of Revisionism* (1982). *The Anxiety of Influence* (1973) sets forth Professor Bloom's provocative theory of the literary relationships between the great writers and their predecessors. His most recent books include *The American Religion* (1992), *The Western Canon* (1994), *Omens of Millennium: The Gnosis of Angels, Dreams, and Resurrection* (1996), and *Shakespeare: The Invention of the Human* (1998), a finalist for the 1998 National Book Award.

Professor Bloom earned his Ph.D. from Yale University in 1955 and has served on the Yale faculty since then. He is a 1985 MacArthur Foundation Award recipient, served as the Charles Eliot Norton Professor of Poetry at Harvard University in 1987–88, and has received honorary degrees from the universities of Rome and Bologna. In 1999, Professor Bloom received the prestigious American Academy of Arts and Letters Gold Medal for Criticism.

Currently, Harold Bloom is the editor of numerous Chelsea House volumes of literary criticism, including the series BLOOM'S NOTES, BLOOM'S MAJOR SHORT STORY WRITERS, BLOOM'S MAJOR POETS, MAJOR LITERARY CHARACTERS, MODERN CRITICAL VIEWS, MODERN CRITICAL INTERPRETATIONS, AND WOMEN WRITERS OF ENGLISH AND THEIR WORKS.

Editor's Note

Among the many Shavian critics represented in the Critical Extracts are Nicholas Grene, Leon Hugo, Alfred Turco Jr., Sidney P. Albert, Daniel Dervin, Jean Reynolds, Louis Crompton, Margery M. Morgan, Charles A. Berst, Judi Dench, Robert Cox, and J. L. Wisenthal. Shaw's own comments on each play are beyond price, good as his exegetes tend to be. One could argue that Shaw's prefaces and correspondence frequently are more absorbing than the plays themselves; perhaps indeed *they* are the true dramas.

Introduction

HAROLD BLOOM

I

The Plays surveyed in this little volume were composed from 1903 to 1923, and represent George Bernard Shaw in his dramatic prime. *Man and Superman* (1903) is in some danger now of seeming a period piece, while *Major Barbara* (1905) is also somewhat dated, despite its effective transformation into a classic of British cinema. The best of Shaw's comedies, *Pygmalion* (1912), also became a celebrated film and is most famous as the musical *My Fair Lady*. *Saint Joan* (1923) seems to me wholly problematical; its heroine undergoes transformations that are not psychologically persuasive. Shaw, who professed to despise Shakespeare, badly needed even an iota of Shakespeare's oceanic capacity for representing human personality and character. A dramatist of ideas (other men's ideas), Shaw rarely understood or appreciated Shakespeare's invention of the human. Ibsen, however ruefully, went to school with Shakespeare, and created *Brand, Peer Gynt, Hedda Gabler*. Shaw, who sought to imitate Ibsen, sketched ideograms and called them characters.

II

Man and Superman lives today only in its interlude, *Don Juan in Hell*. How odd it would be to say that *Hamlet* lives only in *The Mousetrap*, the Prince of Denmark's revision of the supposed *Murder of Gonzago* into the play-within-a-play whose purpose is to affright the conscience of the usurper, Claudius. But then Hamlet is perhaps the greatest of all literary-dramatic characters, while *Man and Superman*'s hero, John Tanner, is precisely what Eric Bentley calls him: "a brilliant gasbag." Shaw, in a stage direction, called his heroine, Ann Whitefield, "a vital genius." That would suffice as a description of Hedda Gabler (of whom Ann Whitefield is a muted imitation), but I'm afraid that Ann Whitefield is a perfect match for Tanner, since she might well be termed: "a vitalistic windbag." Sally Peters, doing the best one can with Shaw's heroine, defends her as myth or archetype, Woman Incarnate or Everywoman. Doubtless that was Shaw's intention, but on stage a mythic windbag is not any more entertaining than is her male quarry, the gasbag Tanner. It would be cruel to ask any reader to juxtapose Ann's speeches with those of Rosalind in *As You Like It*, but the contrast would be forever instructive.

Still, there is *Don Juan in Hell*, the shrewdest work of a crafty ironist. Tanner, Shaw's Don Juan, is something of a Shavian self-parody, and yet achieves authentic eloquence in his debate with the Devil, a person not at all Miltonic-Satanic, but rather a Paterian-Wildean aesthete. Shaw's Don Juan is scarcely amorous, and is an emblem both of Faust and Prometheus. Intellectual debate is difficult to dramatize, but *Don Juan in Hell* still stages effectively, unlike much of the rest of *Man and Superman*.

III

Shaw's peculiar religion of power, which he confused with Creative Evolution, is enshrined in *Major Barbara*, where Barbara yields to her father Undershaft's strength of will. Whether we are to think of Undershaft finally as a benign capitalist or a warlike socialist is quite ambiguous; Shaw's politics were peculiar, and might be termed a Fabian Stalinism. *Major Barbara* is farce, and too easily can be over-interpreted. Barbara's conversion to her father's enterprise has in it a dark element of regression, and makes her childlike again. It should be observed of *Major Barbara* that it does not so much subdue Eros to Creative Will, as it reabsorbs Eros into what Freud called "Family Romances." Barbara, thinking that she still loves and serves God the Father, actually ends loving and serving Undershaft the Father.

IV

Pygmalion, a romance rather than a farce, nevertheless has farcical characters, particularly Professor Higgins, the best of Shaw's many self-parodies. A failed Prometheus, Higgins cannot see that Eliza's vitality is anything but his gift to her. Shaw would not have been pleased that *My Fair Lady* concludes by pairing Higgins and Eliza with one another. In an epilogue to *Pygmalion*, Shaw wickedly married Eliza to Freddy, while insisting that the relation between Eliza and Higgins remained rather cold and formal, a conclusion now intolerable to a public delighted perpetually by *My Fair Lady*. Shaw put it adroitly: "Galatea never does quite like Pygmalion; his relation to her is too godlike to be agreeable."

V

Saint Joan is taken to be Shaw's masterpiece at tragicomedy, but its inconsistencies remain troublesome. Joan is both a firm Protestant and a Shavian vitalist, and she never invokes Jesus Christ or the Virgin Mary. For her, the Will of God simply is her own will, and she ends as Shaw's own substitute for Jesus: Joan of Arc becomes the Divine Daughter of the Life Force. And like the Life Force, Joan has no personality. She is not a coherent psyche; you cannot link the girl of the opening scenes to the heroine who repudiates her own recantation, or to the ghostly saint of the play's epilogue. Shaw's ironies partly sustain the drama, but Joan finally is more an idea than a person. ✾

Biography of
George Bernard Shaw

George Bernard Shaw, third child and only son of George Carr Shaw and Lucinda Elizabeth Gurly Shaw, was born in Dublin on July 26, 1856. The Shaw family was of Anglo-Irish heritage and belonged to the upper middle-class Protestant section of Irish society.

Later in his life, Shaw would often write about the difficulities he faced as a youth because of the incompatibility of his father and mother. His father was a weak man who was unsuccessful at his business; apparently he was also an alcoholic. His mother was disillusioned and disgusted with her husband, but when she married she had been disowned by her own family. As a result, she had no choice but to stay with him. The three children, wrote Shaw, were brought up mainly by neglectful servants.

In 1862, the Shaws moved in with Mrs. Shaw's music teacher, George John Vandeleur Lee. Lee organized concerts and operas, and he made use of Mrs. Shaw's talents as singer, chorus leader, and organizer. Mr. Lee became the head of their household, but according to Shaw, his father never seemed to resent this. Throughout his life, Shaw maintained that Lee did not have an adulterous relationship with his mother.

At the age of fifteen, after attending several different schools, Shaw began his first job as office boy and later clerk for Uniacke Townshend and Company, a firm of estate agents in Dublin. Mrs. Shaw and her two daughters moved with Lee to London in 1872, while Shaw remained with his father in Dublin. Five years later, fearing that he could never achieve his literary ambitions in Dublin, Shaw joined his sister Lucy and their mother in London.

Initially Shaw was uncomfortable and self-conscious in London. To combat this, he joined several debate teams and became active in public political discussions. But the next several years were difficult professionally for Shaw, who wrote five unsuccessful novels during this time. As a consequence, Shaw had no income for these early trying years.

Nevertheless, during the 1880s, Shaw exposed himself to many varied influences and developed in other ways. He became a vegetarian, following the example of poet Percy Shelley. After hearing the American economist Henry George speak, Shaw became a socialist, and in 1884, when he met Beatrice and Sidney Webb, Shaw joined the new Fabian Society, a socialist organization. To expand his understanding of socialism, he read Karl Marx's *Das Kapital.*

Politically, Shaw remained true to the Fabian Society's moderate understanding of socialism. This less extreme viewpoint was reinforced when Shaw witnessed the violence of the police and troops brought in to break up the socialist protest in London on what became known as Bloody Sunday, November 13, 1887. This event apparently convinced Shaw that force was ineffective, causing him to turn instead to debate and drama to educate others in socialist thought. Shaw began to make a mark in literary circles around this time, with the publication of *The Quintessence of Ibsenism* in 1891.

Earlier, Shaw had begun an eight-year relationship with Mrs. Jenny Patterson, a widow who was 15 years his senior. Although Shaw drew much from this relationship, his next mistress, the actress Florence Farr, more clearly characterized the New Woman, a figure to appear often in Shaw's work. Of the other women in his life, Ellen Terry stands out because of the correspondence she and Shaw shared for twenty-six years. Although Shaw only met Terry twice in his life, the tone of their correspondence at times was similar to love letters.

Through his Fabian friends Beatrice and Sidney Webb, Shaw met Charlotte Payne-Townshend, an Irish millionaire. They began to exchange love letters. A little later, Shaw injured his foot and was forced to stay home for some time. When Charlotte came to visit, she reacted so strongly to the poor conditions in which Shaw was living—clutter, grime, plates of half-eaten food, stacks of books and papers—that she decided he should move to an apartment she had rented. Once there, Shaw insisted that Charlotte get them a marriage license. They were married on June 1, 1898, in a civil ceremony; however many believe the marriage remained unconsummated. In the same year, Shaw wrote *Caesar and Cleopatra.*

One test to the strength of the marriage came in the person of Mrs. Patrick Campbell. At the end of the 19th century, when Shaw was already a successful playwright, Mrs. Campbell was a renowned actress who caught Shaw's attention. He wanted Mrs. Campbell in his plays and began a correspondence that, on Shaw's part at least, may not have been entirely limited to professional interests. Nevertheless, Mrs. Campbell spurned Shaw's pursuits, and Charlotte and Shaw remained married until her death at the age of 86 in 1943.

Throughout his life, Shaw's relationships with women were slightly odd, to say the least. The prudishness of Victorian England was exaggerated among the Irish, and Shaw, like other Irish writers such as James Joyce and W. B. Yeats, grew up in an atmosphere that elevated the intellect while looking with repulsion at the physical. This attitude influenced the work of the Irish writers—and without a doubt, it also influenced their personal lives. In Shaw's case, he was easily infatuated with members of the opposite sex, and his plays portray a sexuality that ends in the fulfillment and productivity of marriage—but in his own life, his relationships with women never produced this kind of physical and intellectual fulfillment. As a child, he did not live in a home where he witnessed this sort of union, and as an adult, he was apparently incapable of achieving it himself.

As Shaw became more involved in political thought, his success in the theater also increased. After his early plays in the late 1880s, he continued to write and produce prolifically until the year of his death. Shaw also participated actively in the production of his works. For the preparation of his works, Shaw told actresses how to deliver their lines, commented on scenery, and provided extensive background information in the prefaces and stage directions of his plays. He confronted censors who refused to issue a permit for *Mrs. Warren's Profession* in 1893. The London production of *Man and Superman* in 1905, which omitted the *Don Juan in Hell* dream sequence, marked the beginning of his most important period. That same year, *Major Barbara* opened at the Royal Court Theatre. Shaw also opened his plays outside of England quite often; for example, *Pygmalion* was first produced in Vienna in 1913, and *Heartbreak House* and *Saint Joan* opened in New York in 1916 and 1923, respectively. The last Shaw play to be produced was *Buoyant Billions,* which opened in Zurich in October of 1948.

In his works, Shaw criticized almost everything identifiable with English society. He was critical of the English participation in World War I (*Commonsense about the War,* 1914) and was sympathetic to the Irish 1916 rebellion. His writing also criticizes the failures of capitalism. In 1923, Shaw refused a knighthood, but he did accept the Nobel Prize in 1925. Despite his many criticisms of life around him, Shaw believed in a natural man who could improve himself by means of correct social awareness combined with the energy Shaw thought emanated from a universal Life Force.

Shaw was convinced that people could live as long as they wished, so long as they were in tune with their own bodies and the Life Force. He intended to prove that it could be done—but when he was 93, he fell out of a tree he was pruning and broke his hip. When his doctor informed him that his hip would not heal, leaving him helpless, Shaw replied that he did not choose to live like that. He died within the week, on November 2, 1950. ❀

Plot Summary of
Man and Superman

The first production of *Man and Superman* was held at the Royal Court Theatre in London in May of 1905. The play, which Shaw subtitled "A Comedy and a Philosophy," contains four acts. A text written by the fictitious John Tanner, called "The Revolutionist's Handbook," also appears in the published editions of the play.

Act I opens in the study of Roebuck Ramsden, an older man visibly tied to a previous generation. He is at his writing table when the parlormaid announces the arrival of Octavius Robinson. Much younger and quite attractive, Robinson is dressed in black clothes of bereavement. Ramsden welcomes him and expresses condolences at his loss. They exchanges favorable remarks about the dead man, Mr. Whitefield, who in life was a close friend of Ramsden and who considered Octavius a son. They speak of the dead man's daughters and Ramsden assures Octavius that Whitefield would want the young man to step in and marry Ann Whitefield, the older girl. Octavius would like nothing else, but he is unsure of her wishes.

Ramsden sees only one impediment: the existence of John Tanner, Ann's friend since childhood, a man he considers thoroughly unacceptable. While Ramsden points out at length Tanner's faults, Tanner suddenly comes into the room uninvited and unannounced. He holds a copy of Whitefield's will, in which Ramsden and Tanner are both appointed Ann's guardians. The two men are equally shocked. Ramsden wants no part of such an association. Tanner sees the appointment as a moral compromise. He insists that Octavius should marry Ann, thus freeing him from such a constricting responsibility. When Octavius suggests that they seek Ann's opinion, Tanner replies: "Ann will do exactly what she likes. And whats more, she'll force us to advise her to do it; and she'll put the blame on us if it turns out badly."

They ask Ann, who has been upstairs with her mother, to join them. Ramsden expresses his grief at her loss but then turns his comments to the unusual arrangement noted in the will. Ann adopts the position that she must follow her father's wishes and keep both men as close to her as possible. Stating that she is too inexperienced to decide, she appeals to them coyly. Ramsden falls under her control, but Tanner continues to protest. When Octavius complains of Tanner's harsh words against Ann, Tanner expands on what he sees as her true nature as a woman:

TANNER: . . . It is the self-sacrificing women that sacrifice others most recklessly. Because they are unselfish, they are kind in little things. Because they have a purpose which is not their own purpose, but that of the whole universe, a man is nothing to them but an instrument of that purpose.

OCTAVIUS: Dont be ungenerous, Jack. They take the tenderest care of us.

TANNER: Yes, as a soldier takes care of his rifle or a musician of his violin. But do they allow us any purpose or freedom of our own? Will they lend us to one another? Can the strongest man escape from them when once he is appropriated?

Octavius does not share Tanner's cynical views.

Much of the comedy in this play comes from the fact that Tanner is Ann's real prey, while Tanner, unaware of Ann's designs, tries his best to save Octavius from Ann's clutches.

After spending some time outside the study, Ramsden and Ann return to deliver unsettling news to Octavius. Ramsden reluctantly reveals that his sister Violet did not visit friends as she had announced; instead, Violet was seen at a doctor's office wearing a wedding ring. Even worse, Violet has not run away with her shame; she is in the housekeeper's room at Ramsden's house and refuses to give any details. Ann reports that her mother and Ramsden's spinster sister are considering what should be done.

Tanner convinces Octavius to seek out his sister and speak with her. In the meantime, Ramsden and Tanner exchange barbs. Ann asks Ramsden to intercede with the ladies upstairs. He goes to do this and leaves her alone with Tanner. Ann begins to reminisce about their shared childhood confidences. Tanner resentfully accuses her of luring him to reveal secrets when they were children. He argues that he stopped sharing with her because he developed a soul and a sense of duty. The birth of passion turned him into a man, Tanner contends, explaining that "the moral passion made our childish relations impossible. A jealous sense of my new individuality arose in me. . . . " Ann accuses him of vanity but Tanner considers it emancipation from her control.

TANNER: . . . Even then you had acquired that damnable woman's trick of heaping obligations on a man, of placing yourself so entirely and helplessly at his mercy that at last he dare not take a step without running to you for leave. . . . If we try to go where you do not want us to go there is no law to prevent us; but when we take the first step your breasts are under our foot as it descends: your bodies are under our wheels as we start. No woman shall ever enslave me in that way.

Ann tries to charm him, nevertheless. But Tanner now wishes Ramsden would return to protect him from her whims.

Just then Ramsden and Octavius come back with Miss Ramsden. The conversation turns again to the case of Violet. When she joins them, Violet refuses to tell them anything and has ordered a cab so that she can leave the house. Tanner openly supports Violet, announcing to her that he thinks she is in the right. Violet reacts indignantly:

> VIOLET: Oh! You think me a wicked woman, like the rest. You think I have not only been vile, but that I share your abominable opinions.
> MISS RAMSDEN: I have borne your hard words because I knew you would be sorry for them when you found out the truth. But I wont bear such a horrible insult as to be complimented by Jack on being one of the wretches of whom he approves. I have kept my marriage a secret for my husband's sake. But now I claim my right as a married woman not to be insulted.

All are shocked except Ann, who was aware of Violet's news all along. Violet goes on with her verbal attack on the others. When she exits, she leaves them with their opinions as the scene ends.

The scene shifts in **Act II** to the country, where Tanner and his chauffeur Straker are talking about Tanner's touring car. Straker is a crack mechanic but Tanner becomes frustrated by talking to Straker's legs as he works under the car. They are joined by Octavius, who has come with Ann and his sister Violet in another car driven by an American named Malone. As the three men talk, Tanner points out that Straker is quite arrogant:

> TANNER: . . . He positively likes the car to break down because it brings out my gentlemanly helplessness and his workmanlike skill and resource.
> STRAKER: Never you mind him, Mr. Robinson. He likes to talk. We know him, dont we?
> OCTAVIUS: But theres a great truth at the bottom of what he says. I believe most intensely in the dignity of labor.
> STRAKER: Thats because you never done any, Mr. Robinson. My business is to do away with labor. Youll get more out of me and a machine than you will out of twenty laborers, and not so much to drink either.

Straker goes back to tending the car, while Tanner and Octavius change the topic of conversation to Ann. The night before, Octavius proposed to her but Ann put him off by saying that he must first consult her guardians. Reacting to this comment, Tanner launches into another lecture on women: "Why, man, what other work has she in life but to get a husband? It is a woman's business to get married as soon as possible, and a man's to keep unmarried as long as he can." Octavius insists that his poetry will suffer without Ann. He contends that Tanner does not understand his predicament because Tanner has never been in love. To the contrary, Tanner explains; he *is* in love with Ann also but intends never to become a slave of love.

Then Octavius remembers he has a letter from Rhoda, Ann's younger sister, to deliver to Tanner. In the letter, Rhoda reports that Ann has forbidden her to be alone with Tanner. The letter makes Tanner irate. Ann joins them then and makes excuses for her sister, saying that Rhoda has a terrible headache. Tanner feels vindicated by Ann's fabrication, but Octavius does not get the point; he is too enamored with Ann. She sends Octavius off to be with her mother. Tanner asks her to explain the real reason for her sister's absence. Ann reports that she is merely obeying her mother's wishes. Reacting cynically again, Tanner invites her to break her chains of responsibility and accompany him on a trip to North Africa in his motor car. He is aghast when Ann accepts his invitation.

Tanner's uncomfortable situation is interrupted by the arrival of Mrs. Whitefield, Ramsden, and Octavius. Hector Malone, the American, also joins them. Ann tells her mother of Tanner's invitation; Tanner is surprised at her immediate acceptance of the idea. Ann introduces Tanner to Malone, who wants to extend the travel plans to include Violet Robinson. Ann and her mother leave the men to discuss the details.

Octavius objects to Violet's going on the trip. Tanner explains to Malone the delicate situation of Violet's clandestine marriage. Octavius and Ramsden reluctantly supply the few details known about Violet's secret. Ramsden, Tanner, and Octavius then leave Malone. Violet soon joins him. Checking that no one can see them, they kiss. They talk about Hector's father and their need to keep their marriage a secret, since Mr. Malone would disown his son if the marriage were discovered. They go off together.

Tanner and Straker return. Tanner asks Straker to help Octavius spend as much time with Ann as possible. Straker tells him that Ann is not interested in Octavius but in Tanner. At the idea of being Ann's prey, Tanner begs Straker to make haste and take him to "any port from which we can sail to a Mahometan country where men are protected from women." The scene ends as they speed off in the car.

A radical shift in location takes place as **Act III** opens. In the Sierra Nevada in the south of Spain, a group of brigands gathers near a fire in an abandoned quarry that commands a view of the valley and the road below. The leader, who speaks English, addresses his company. They have spent three evenings discussing the principles of Anarchism and Social Democracy. He asks that they treat each other as gentlemen. The goatherd in the group spots a car approaching, and the band jumps into action. They have already sprinkled nails on the road; they plan to shoot out a tire if necessary.

The automobile in question belongs to Tanner and Straker. Mendoza, the leader of the brigands, makes the necessary introductions:

> MENDOZA: Allow me to introduce myself: Mendoza, President of the League of the Sierra! I am a brigand: I live by robbing the rich.
> TANNER: I am a gentleman: I live by robbing the poor. Shake hands.

After clarifying that his men will not interfere with the car, Mendoza dismisses them and invites Tanner and Straker to sit by the fire. Tanner assures Mendoza that he is rich enough to pay any ransom. Although he is surprised at this frankness, Mendoza reacts favorably. Tanner asks if the men are all socialists. Mendoza is quick to explain that they are brigands:

> MENDOZA: . . . Brigandage is abnormal. Abnormal professions attract two classes: those who are not good enough for ordinary bourgeois life and those who are too good for it. We are dregs and scum, sir: the dregs very filthy, the scum very superior.

Mendoza proceeds to tell the two men the story of how he, a former waiter and quite cosmopolitan, became a brigand in the Sierra Nevada. He was in love with a woman of humor, intellect, and good cooking skills. She was a worker like Mendoza but refused to marry him because he is a Jew. As the story unfolds, it becomes clear that Mendoza is speaking of Straker's sister Louisa.

> STRAKER: Look here: Louisa Straker is my sister, see? Wot do you mean by gassing about her like this? Wot she got to do with you?
> MENDOZA: A dramatic coincidence! You are Enry, her favorite brother!

STRAKER: Oo are you callin Enry? What call have you to take a liberty with my name or with hers? For two pins I'd punch your fat edd, so I would.
MENDOZA: If I let you do it, will you promise to brag of it afterwards to her? She will be reminded of her Mendoza: that is all I desire.

Tanner finally calms down Straker, who turns away from them and settles down to sleep near the fire.

Mendoza continues to tell Tanner of his love for Louisa. He produces a manuscript written in her honor, but Tanner advises him to throw it in the fire. Mendoza pleads with Tanner to let him read from the manuscript. The verse dedicated to Louisa puts Tanner to sleep. A dejected Mendoza talks himself to sleep by repeating Louisa's name.

An even more drastic location change takes place as the dream sequence begins. Don Juan, looking much like John Tanner, speaks to an old woman who meets him in Hell. As it turns out, she is Doña Ana, one of the many women Don Juan seduced while alive. She attacks him verbally for causing the death of her father, Don Gonzalo. But Don Juan informs her that her father is in Heaven.

DON JUAN: He condescends to look in upon us here from time to time. Heaven bores him. So let me warn you that if you meet him he will be mortally offended if you speak of me as his murderer! He maintains that he was a much better swordsman than I . . . I never dispute the point; so we are excellent friends.

As they talk about Don Gonzalo, Mozart's statue music, as Don Juan calls it, announces the arrival of Don Gonzalo in statue form.

Don Juan has to introduce the statue to the daughter he has forgotten. But instead of talking to Ana, Don Gonzalo asks where their friend the Devil has been. When the Devil arrives, he talks with Don Juan and the statue. Don Juan prefers to be alone so the Devil suggests that he take refuge in Heaven. Doña Ana is now very confused.

ANA: But why doesnt everybody go to Heaven, then?
THE STATUE: *I* can tell you that, my dear. It's because Heaven is the most angelically dull place in all creation: thats why.
THE DEVIL: His excellency the Commander puts it with military bluntness; but the strain of living in Heaven is intolerable. There is a notion that I was turned out of it; but as a matter of fact nothing could have induced me to stay there. I simply left it and organized this place.

The ensuing discussion allows the three men, in the majority, to debate a number of philosophical and political issues: stupidity and imagination, human greed and sloth, the Catholic Church and Islam, and men and women.

When challenged by Doña Ana about his views on women, Don Juan declares:

> Sexually, Woman is Nature's contrivance for perpetuating its highest achievement. Sexually, Man is Woman's contrivance for fulfilling Nature's behest in the most economical way. She knows by instinct that far back in the evolutionary process she invented him, differentiated him, created him in order to produce something better than the single-sexed process can produce. Whilst he fulfills his purpose for which she made him, he is welcome to his dreams . . . provided that the keystone of them all is the worship of women.

The debate moves on to the subject of marriage. Ana maintains that "most marriages are perfectly comfortable." Don Juan responds: "Those who talk most about the blessings of marriage and the constancy of its vows are the very people who declare that if the chain were broken and the prisoners left free to choose, the whole social fabric would fly asunder. You cannot have the argument both ways. If the prisoner is happy, why lock him in? If he is not, why pretend that he is?"

The Devil becomes more active in the debate when Don Juan insists on discussing the Life Force, which, according to him, gives one the chance to steer in life instead of drifting. The Devil encourages Don Juan to go his own way. They all part as Don Juan seeks the way to Heaven.

Turner and Mendoza wake up when they hear shouts from the road. They both comment that they had amazing dreams, but the approach of another automobile attracts everyone's attention. As it turns out, it is Malone's car. Octavius and Ramsden have come along with Ann, Violet, and Hector. Ann has successfully tracked down Tanner as the scene ends.

In **Act IV,** the location is the garden of an expensive villa in Granada near the Alhambra. Straker is talking to an elderly gentleman, Hector Malone, their conversation a bit strained. Violet interrupts and asks Straker if he has delivered his letter for her. As it turns out, Straker tried to deliver the letter, but Mr. Hector Malone took the letter intended for his son. Mr. Malone asks to speak with Violet. Because Malone has read the letter, Violet feels unable to hide the truth, but she only tells Mr. Malone that Hector has asked her to marry him. Mr. Malone does not object to the news, but he makes it clear that his son will do so without any financial support from his father.

As they continue their conversation, Hector the son arrives. He attacks his father for opening a confidential letter not addressed to him. They quarrel even after the arrival of Tanner and Ramsden, followed by Ann and Octavius. Hector refuses to introduce the others to his father. The others are confused by his behavior and that of Violet. The conversation becomes agitated and insults begin to fly. Hector finally announces that Violet is his wife. Furthermore, Hector gives back the stipend his father had given him and declares that he will work for his living. Hector departs with the others, leaving Violet with his father. Violet is upset by the discussion and intends to pack her belongings. Before she leaves, however, Violet tells Mr. Malone that she will take the money Hector refused. She also advises him not to buy any of the houses he had described to her until she is able to check them. Tanner and Ramsden witness Violet's behavior and Tanner comments: "And that poor devil is a billionaire! One of the master spirits of the age! Led in a string like a pug dog by the first girl who takes the trouble to despise him! I wonder will it ever come to that with me."

In the garden, Octavius tells Ann that his heart belongs to her. But Ann declares that her mother has decided that Tanner is the man for her daughter. Octavius reluctantly accepts reality, but still he pledges Ann his love forever. Octavius asks if he should tell Tanner of Ann's decision:

> ANN: Oh no: he'd run away again.
> OCTAVIUS: Ann: would you marry an unwilling man?
> ANN: What a queer creature you are, Tavy! Theres no such thing as a willing man when you really go for him. . . .

She leaves him to sulk as Mrs. Whitefield comes in. She finds him crying. Mrs. Whitefield guesses what Ann has told him and tells Octavius that Ann follows the wishes of no one but herself. He leaves to wash his face when Tanner returns. Tanner and Mrs. Whitefield face reality:

> MRS. WHITEFIELD: . . . Of course youll marry Ann whether I like it or not—
> TANNER: It seems to me that I shall presently be married to Ann whether I like it myself or not.

They talk frankly to each other and outline Ann's faults. But Mrs. Whitefield reaches the conclusion that Tanner is the best choice for her daughter.

When Ann and Tanner find themselves alone, Tanner declares: "Ann: I will not marry you. Do you hear? I wont, wont, wont, wont, WONT marry you" He further announces to her:

> Marriage is to me apostasy, profanation of the sanctuary of my soul, violation of my manhood, sale of my birthright, shameful surrender, ignominious capitulation, acceptance of defeat. I shall decay like a thing that has served its purpose and is done with; I shall change from a man with a future to a man with a past . . . to the women I, who have always been an enigma and a possibility, shall be merely somebody else's property—and damaged goods at that: a secondhand man at best.

Ann is unchanged by Tanner's barrage. Tanner concludes that he is in "the grip of the Life Force." But by her cunning, Ann gets Tanner to confess that he loves her. As the others return, Ann says that she is about to faint. When asked why, she declares that she has promised to marry Tanner. She is successful in convincing all present that Tanner has asked her to marry him. Tanner finally acquiesces and announces the wedding plans to all as the play ends.

If *Man and Superman* was produced in its entirety, it would run for six hours. However, Act III—the dream sequence with Don Juan—is almost always omitted. *Don Juan in Hell* is often offered by itself as a full-length play.

The play was popular with viewers, for it offered them the traditional "happily ever after," with all of the lovers matched at the end as the viewers had hoped from the beginning. Much of the play's humor came from the idea that the male is actually the pursued, while the female is the pursuer, a role reversal that was humorously novel at the time of the play's writing. The happy ending affirms the union of the sexes through marriage. ❀

List of Characters in
Man and Superman

An older gentleman of conservative beliefs, **Roebuck Ramsden** disapproves of Tanner and his philosophical posturing. Reluctantly, Ramsden must share the guardianship of Ann with Tanner. Ramsden regularly offers his opinion in opposition to that of Tanner.

Octavius Robinson, Tavy for short, is in love with Ann although her attentions are directed elsewhere. He is a sincere young fellow who cannot see through Ann's cunning ways.

A philosopher and staunch supporter of bachelorhood, **John Tanner** unwillingly becomes Ann's guardian. He maintains throughout that Woman has designs to trap Man and control him. Tanner does whatever possible not to fall into Ann's trap.

Henry Straker, Tanner's chauffeur, is an expert mechanic who enjoys driving fast. He is proud to be a self-sufficient man.

A young American, **Hector Malone**, has married Violet Robinson in secret for fear that his father will disown him.

An elderly Irishman, **Mr. Malone**, has made a great fortune in the furniture business. He is the father of Hector Malone, and disapproves of his son's marriage to Violet.

Ann Whitefield is a young woman whose guardianship falls to Tanner and Ramsden because of her father's will. Ann appears obedient on the outside but really is a woman of determined will with definite plans for her future. She plays along with Octavius and Tanner but has decided from the beginning to marry Jack Tanner.

Mrs. Whitefield, the widow, accepts the dictates of her husband's will. Ann uses her mother as an excuse when it suits her.

Miss Ramsden is Ramsden's spinster sister who runs his household. Miss Ramsden steps in when Violet comes to their home in the middle of a scandal.

Violet Robinson, Octavius's sister, causes scandal among the group when they find out she has married in secret. Violet, unlike Ann, declares her opinion directly to the others. She stands by her husband Hector when he decides to work for his living.

The chief of the brigands who robs passersby, **Mendoza** was a waiter and left England when the love of his life, Louisa, refused to marry him.

The **Three Social-Democrats** are a Frenchman, a Rowdy Englishman, and a Solemn Englishman

Don Juan is Tanner's dream counterpart

Doña Ana is Ann Whitefield's dream persona

Don Gonzalo, the Statue, is Ramsden as the Commander in the dream

The Devil is Mendoza in the dream sequence ❀

Critical Views on
Man and Superman

GEORGE BERNARD SHAW ON THE STAGING OF THE PLAY

[In this letter to actress Lillah McCarthy, Shaw offers stage directions and suggestions to improve her timing on stage, based on the matinée performance of *Man and Superman* he attended at the Royal Court on June 6, 1905. Granville Barker played John Tanner, Lewis Casson played Octavius, and Dame Edith S. Lyttelton later served with Shaw on the Executive Committee of the Shakespeare Memorial National Theatre. Although he praises McCarthy's performance, Shaw's direction clearly indicates his involvement with the production of his plays.]

To LILLAH McCARTHY

10 Adelphi Terrace W C
7th June 1905

My dear Miss Lillah

I was in front on Tuesday, and noticed a point or two of importance to you.

In the third act, when Malone, Ramsden & Tanner go off making a great cackle & fuss, do not begin the scene with Tavy until the noise is over and the audience's attention has quite come back to you. Just wait, looking provokingly at Tavy, until there is a dead silence & expectation & then say, without the least hurry, "Wont you go with them, Tavy?" Otherwise you will not get the new key and the slow movement.

At the end when you say "I want to make you cry for the last time" say it to Tavy alone: the others are not supposed to hear it: it is one of Anne's wicked asides.

Dont forget to say "but you nearly killed me, Jack, for all that" as if you meant it. He *has* nearly killed you. Mrs. Lyttelton, close behind me, explained to her party that Ann was only pretending to faint. That is not exactly true. Ann doesnt faint exactly, but she does collapse from utter exhaustion after her "daring so frightfully."

It was one of the best performances I have seen you do.

Why did you come on on your wrong side after the wait? If it occurs again, dont hurry: go round and come on with aggravating leisureliness. I was unfeeling enough to shake with laughter at poor Barker & Casson.

yrs ever

G. Bernard Shaw

—George Bernard Shaw, Letter to Lillah McCarthy, 7 June 1905, in *Bernard Shaw: Collected Letters Vol 2: 1898–1910*, ed. Dan H. Laurence (New York: Viking, 1985): p. 528.

⊛

EDWARD V. GEIST ON ANN WHITEFIELD AND HEDDA GABLER

[Edward V. Geist, an assistant professor at Hofstra University, has also written on John Dryden. In this essay, Geist proposes a comparison of the principal female characters in *Man and Superman* and Ibsen's *Hedda Gabler* to suggest that Shaw used Ibsen's Hedda as a pattern for Ann Whitefield.]

Man and Superman is rich in its echoes of other works. If Shaw borrowed the plot twists and turns from the well-made play, he looked to other works for the more serious elements in his play. For the character of Ann Whitefield, he cites in the "Epistle Dedicatory" the "fifteenth century Dutch morality called Everyman" (*Man and Superman* xxviii) as his inspiration, his aim being to create a modern Everywoman. While he may have gained his conception of Ann from Everyman, he built her characterization out of materials that were closer at hand. One source that hitherto has gone unnoticed is Ibsen's *Hedda Gabler*. Here we have a classic example of Shavian imitation and transformation. Shaw gives Ann a character and background similar to Hedda's, but these similarities are not likely be noticed by an audience since Ann is apparently free of the neurotic anxiety which we associate with Hedda Gabler.

Shaw describes Ann as one of the "vital geniuses" of humanity (*Man and Superman* 15), a unique blend of mind and will. She is a classic example of a Shavian "new woman"—one who obeys "like a man the law of her own nature" rather than "like a dutiful daughter the law of her father's nature" (Watson 158). Hedda Gabler is anything but a new woman. Her existence is marked by frustration and defeat. Harold Clurman finds "social position" (163) the key element in her characterization, describing her as "a passionate being in a society where marrying a 'wild poet' was unthinkable and an affair with a known debauchee scandalous" (162). Her marriage to Joergen Tesman—a weak, ineffectual pedant—is an act of desperation, and she dreads the thought of impending motherhood. In contrast, Ann Whitefield has a purpose to fulfill—to marry Jack Tanner and to have her children by him. We never doubt that Ann will achieve her goal, no matter what the conventions of a class society may dictate.

Despite these obvious differences, the similarities between these two characters are remarkable enough to indicate that Shaw patterned certain aspects of Ann's characterization after Hedda Gabler. First off, we should note that their backgrounds are similar. Both have lost their fathers, and they are treated by most of the other characters like delicate, sensitive creatures whose every whim must be attended to. The male characters in particular fuss about their comfort and security as if they were incapable of looking after themselves.

—Edward V. Geist, "Ann Whitefield and Hedda Gabler: Two Versions of Everywoman." *The Independent Shavian* 24, no 2–3 (Summer–Fall 1986): pp. 27–28.

⟨᠗⟩

BARBARA BELLOW WATSON ON FEMINIST CRITICISM
OF *MAN AND SUPERMAN*

[Barbara Bellow Watson is director of the Women's Studies Program at the City University of New York. Her books include *A Shavian Guide to the Intelligent Woman* and *Women's Studies: The Social Realities*. In this essay, Professor Watson examines the structure of Shaw's comedy, discussing why *Man and Superman* is problematic for feminist critics.]

Man and Superman seems to be the chief stumbling block for feminists approaching Shaw. Here, of course, the outline of the plot is conventional to the point of parody. The curtain does indeed come down on one engagement announced, one secret marriage accepted. Ann does employ feminine wiles to get her man. And the author does in the Epistle Dedicatory speak of Woman as mother and say that "Ann is Everywoman." All this looks like male chauvinism and also like classic comedy. But not quite. Without taking the technical out provided by the author's saying this is "not a play, but a volume which contains a play." It is still possible to see an essential difference from traditional comedy, the very difference that the inclusion of the woman's viewpoint makes.

The pursuit of matrimony, running but never smooth, is again the center of the comic pattern. Octavius woos Ann, who woos Jack Tanner, who regards marriage as apostasy. Violet and Hector are secretly married and wooing Hector's father for support. Feminists naturally object to the implication that marriage is the natural goal of a woman's life, ignoring the fact that both Octavius and young Hector are as dedicated to that goal as the women, and that even Tanner, eloquent as he is on the subject, is no very reliable narrator of his own feelings on marriage or on the more pertinent subject of his feelings about Ann herself. The fact that both male and female are all for love is no departure from convention, but the nature of the obstacles certainly is. The resistance of Tanner, the Don Juan of the piece, is notorious, and his reasons are not very different from those of Shakespeare's Benedict. The resistance of Ann is less evident and more significant. Octavius is the man for whom Ann would be destined in a simpler story, as we know from *Don Giovanni* and from indications supplied by Shaw in his stage directions:

> Mr. Robinson is really an uncommonly nice looking young fellow. He must, one thinks, be the jeune premier; for it is not in reason to suppose that a second such attractive male figure should appear in one story.

Ann herself creates the complications without which there would be no play when she rejects this romantic whole-hearted lover. She does so because she is no longer the heroine of all female flesh and feminine caprice, but a person with ideas and conscious choice, a modern woman. Leaving aside the question of whether "Woman Immortal," one of the more provoking examples of Shavian gamesmanship, is speaking through Ann, as Saint Joan's voices speak through her own unconscious mind, the mere mortal has quite decided ideas as distinct from simple impulses. Another unconventional touch is leaving the attractive Octavius unmated, in spite of the existence of a convenient sister whom any conventional plotting would have worked up into a fiancée. Besides, the sub-plot, with its suitably crasser sub-theme (money), acts as a foil for the high ideas behind the figure of Ann. Violet, named for a flower that is a symbol of feminine modesty but actually grows like a weed, simply wants her Hector and his father's money, which is standard and all right. Empty and attractive, Violet and Hector are the pristine stuff of comedy. Their simplicity hints at the complexity of Ann's motives which are explained in the Epistle Dedicatory.

—Barbara Bellow Watson, "The New Woman and the New Comedy."
The Shaw Review 17, no. 1 (January 1974): pp. 7–8.

⊛

Janie Caves McCauley on "Rikki-Tikki-Tavi" and Shaw's Women

[Janie Caves McCauley, an English professor at the University of Miami, has published articles on Shakespeare and Robert Herrick as well as on Shaw. In this essay, McCauley proposes Kipling's *The Jungle Book,* especially the short story "Rikki-tikki-tavi," as a source Shaw employed when writing *Man and Superman.* The relationships between male and female characters in both works are used to illustrate her thesis.]

Kipling depicts both Nagaina and Darzee's wife as more intelligent and cunning than their mates. Another male animal in the story, Chuchundra the muskrat, is also depicted as a pitifully weak creature who laments the fact that he "never had spirit enough to run out into the middle of the room." Similarly, in *Man and Superman* the male characters are dominated by the females. Ann's authority over Octavius and Ramsden is unquestionable throughout the play, and she uses her feminine powers to gain control over the proud Tanner by the final curtain. Violet Robinson, Tavy's sister and Ann's friend, also dominates the important men in her life.

Unattractive as these domineering females may be, they are not left unmotivated for their crafty means of gaining supremacy over males by either Kipling or Shaw. The female creatures in "Rikki-Tikki-Tavi," like the human Mrs. Bird who is appalled by the idea of her son's sleeping with a mongoose, are driven by a desire to nurture and protect their young. Shaw clearly develops this same idea in *Man and Superman*, where he expounds his philosophy of the Life Force through the mouth of Jack Tanner. This character who eventually becomes the comic victim of the play explains that women "have a purpose which is not their own purpose, but that of the whole universe," man being "nothing to them but an instrument of that purpose." He later identifies this high purpose as "to increase, multiply, and replenish the earth." Like Kipling's female cobra Nagaina, Shaw's Ann Whitefield is described as a snake. In the stage directions Shaw emphasizes that she is "a well formed creature . . . with ensnaring eyes and hair," just as Darzee's wife underlines Nagaina's power to charm a bird with her eyes. Before Ann ever enters the play, Tanner likens her to a boa constrictor. Later as she confronts him directly he ironically exclaims, "I felt the coils tightening around my very self, though you are only playing with me." When Tanner finally realizes that he, not Tavy, is the one whom Ann wants to marry, he says, "Then I—*I* am the bee, the spider, the marked down victim, the destined prey."

—Janie Caves McCauley, "Kipling on Women: A New Source for Shaw." *The Shaw Review* 17, no. 1 (January 1974): pp. 42–43.

NICHOLAS GRENE ON IDEOLOGY IN *MAN AND SUPERMAN*

[Nicholas Grene is the author of *Bernard Shaw: A Critical View*, *Shakespeare's Tragic Imagination*, and *Shakespeare, Jonson, Molière: The Comic Contract*. In this excerpt, he discusses the resonances of Shopenhauer and Nietzsche that he finds in *Man and Superman*.]

It is this purpose of supplying it with an ideology which is the outstandingly original feature of *Man and Superman* as love-comedy. For all the iconoclasm of a Don Juan who is the pursued rather than the pursuer, the comic action of *Man and Superman* is not in itself all that unorthodox. In most love-comedies, even the most romantic, there is an anti-romantic strain implied in the form itself. Love is seen as a blind force controlling the characters, and the comedian exploits the ironic disparity between the apparent individuality of feeling expressed by the lovers and the sense that such feelings are universal and impersonal. The bed-trick, Shakespeare's identical twins, are archetypal devices used to suggest the interchangeability of love-objects. Love, sex and marriage in comedy are parts of a more or less cynically viewed social ritual in which individual impulse works always towards ends which are none of its own. What Shaw identifies as the Life Force in *Man and Superman* is no more than the shaping natural providence implicit in the probable and improbable multiple marriages at the end of so many traditional comedies.

If the idea of a metaphysics for sexual attraction may be derived from Schopenhauer, however, the full theory developed in *Man and Superman* is not. For Schopenhauer, at least in the 'Metaphysics of the Love of the Sexes,' the highest type of love was expressed in the most fully mutual passion, though that passion when consummated was likely to end in unhappy marriage. In Schopenhauer it is the will of the man which meets the intellect of the woman. With Shaw it is the woman who exercises the will, her own and that of the Life Force, and man the intellectual who tries to escape from it. There were, no doubt, personal reasons for Shaw's insistence on this image of the battle of the sexes with the reluctant male and the female aggressor. In *The Philanderer,* already, writing directly out of his own experience, he had developed the figure of the hunted philosopher/hero. But even acknowledging this idiosyncratic bias, John Tanner and Ann Whitefield are not fundamentally out of line with the lovers of traditional comedy. Tanner is the type of the comic figure who defies the power of love and must be humbled into marriage. Ann, superficially docile and conventional, in fact wily and disingenuous in pursuit of her love, corresponds to a certain type of comic heroine. Once again it is not the battle of the sexes in *Man and Superman* which differentiates it from other comedies but Shaw/Tanner's continuous theoretical commentary upon it.

Nietzsche takes over where Schopenhauer leaves off in the ideological structure of *Man and Superman*. If the English language owes the word 'superman' to Shaw, Shaw owed the concept to Nietzsche. According to Schopenhauer the human species itself was infinite; anything beyond it was unthinkable. Indeed the perpetuation of the species which was the implacable object of the will to live manifested in sexual attraction was, for him, a source of despair. Shaw's Life Force may have been based on Schopenhauer's World Will, but its positive evolutionary character was shaped by Samuel Butler, and its ultimate goal was the Nietzschean superman. The revelation of the doctrine of the superman is the main aim of the dream interlude, *Don Juan in Hell*. It is the final philosophic plane which it is the function of comedy to reach. There is no necessary connection between the idea of the Life Force as the motive power of sexual attraction, the duel of the sexes, and the concept of the superman. Yet Shaw welds them into a single ideological pattern. Both man and woman, John Tanner and Ann Whitefield, must serve the Life Force. His reluctance, her aggression are essential attributes of their several roles: he as intellectual, as independent mind, strives to escape from the tyranny of physical love and the personal subjection of marriage; she as the principle of vitality must use him to fulfill her creative purpose. Both together are instruments in the evolution of the race. The individuality and intellectual aspiration which makes Tanner resist marriage is precisely what attracts Ann to him as the 'father for the superman.'

—Nicholas Grene, *Bernard Shaw: A Critical View* (London: MacMillan Press Ltd., 1984): pp. 55–57.

Leon Hugo on the Play's Dream Sequence

[Leon Hugo is the author of *High Caste* and *South of Capricorn*. He has published numerous articles on Shaw and his plays. In this extract, Hugo cites the theater directions for the first production of *Don Juan in Hell*, the long dream sequence in *Man and Superman*, pointing out the operatic elements of the production.]

Henderson reports in a footnote on the first production of this piece in 1907: 'The costumes, designed by Charles Ricketts, R.A., were gorgeous: and there was little movement, the characters looking like jewelled figures pinned against a black velvet back drop.' Ricketts himself recounts that Shaw (who was producing) 'rather approved' a suggestion of his—Ricketts'—that 'at a signal given by Mephistopheles, four gilded [*sic.*] thrones should rise from the floor, to the strains of Mozart's minuet in *Don Giovanni*, a lit chandelier descend from the roof, and the black curtains part before an altar bearing flowers and candles surrounding a gilded Venus de Medici.' Nothing came of this because the Vedrenne-Barker management of the Court Theatre could not allow costs much in excess of a shoe-string, but the fact that Shaw approved is significant. He wrote to Ricketts: 'It seems to me that we (I say 'we' much as an organ-blower uses the plural pronoun when speaking of an organist's performance of a Bach fugue) hit on a most valuable and fascinating stage convention. William Morris used always to say that plays should be performed by four people in conventional costumes, the villain in a red cloak, the father in a bob-wig, etc. etc. etc., and I have always loved Harlequin, Columbine, Sganarelle, etc. in eighteenth-century Italian Comedy and French Chapetre painting. If only we could get a few plays with invisible backgrounds and lovely costumes like that in a suitable theatre, with fairy lights all round the proscenium, there would be no end to the delight of the thing.⟨. . .⟩'

If these snippets of theatre history reveal anything, it is that *Don Juan in Hell* was visualized as akin to opera. The costumes, the black velvet curtains, the unattained but wished for thrones, chandelier, and statue, the absence of movement—in a word, everything the eye lights on fosters those prime illusions of opera, which even the most footling libretto and fiddling score may win to their aid: figures larger than life, momentousness of occasion, elevation of sentiment. The style of opera is as far removed from 'real life' as Ruritania is from Covent Garden market, justifiably removed, because its aesthetic value does not and should not depend on the external fidelity with which it represents nature. It depends on hyperbole and turns a petty story about a consumptive courtesan, or a group of conscienceless Bohemians, or a betrayed husband into an epic; opera is exactly what Dr Johnson called it, 'an exotick and irrational entertainment'; for all this it can be indestructably exciting and completely artistic. Shaw knew; and so he used the convention as being best suited to reflect the magnitude of what were to him the most genuinely heroic themes the intellect of man could conceive.

From visual effects to its sibling, tonal effects; to our hearing the four speakers as the traditional vocal quartet: Ana is soprano, Don Juan tenor, the Devil bass, and the Statue, his Mozartian role usurped by the Devil, fills in the gap as counter-tenor, or alto. There can be no question that this distribution of 'parts' has behind it several deeply considered purposes. Certain 'Mozartian strains' haunt the air as the scene opens and three Mozartian characters take part in the debate, although lack of practice (and Shavian requirements) has done odd things to two Mozartian voices, and a hundred years or more of history (and Shavian philosophy) have done odder things to Mozartian ethics. But of course *Don Juan in Hell,* whilst straightway announcing its reliance on the old formal conventions, relies equally on *Don Giovanni* to show how opposed it is in spirit.

—Leon Hugo, *Bernard Shaw: Playwright and Preacher* (London: Methuen & Co., Ltd., 1971): pp. 128–129.

(ⅴ)

ALFRED TURCO JR. ON IDEALISM IN THE PLAY

[Alfred Turco Jr. teaches English at Wesleyan University; he is also the author of *Shaw: The Neglected Plays* and *Shaw's Moral Vision: The Self and Salvation.* In this extract, Turco discusses Shaw's concept of idealism in *Man and Superman* and how it relates to Shaw's *The Quintessence of Ibsenism.*]

Man and Superman is the first play in which Shaw's belief in the possibility of an *effective* idealism is presented with real conviction. We sense it early, in Tanner's description of the aims of the "artist man" (23–24); but even more striking in the context of Shaw's previous thought is Juan's rebuttal of Satan's famous "force of Death" speech (102–104). Lucifer's tirade need not be quoted: suffice it to remind the reader that it ends with a very Shavian peroration about "justice, duty, patriotism, and all the other isms by which even those who are clever enough to be humanely disposed are persuaded to become the most destructive of all the destroyers" (104). Juan's surprising reply, "Pshaw: all this is old," is followed by an even more surprising explanation. Juan argues that men are cowardly rather than evil, and then goes on to say:

> You can make any of these cowards brave by simply putting an idea into his head. . . . Men never really overcome fear until they imagine they are fighting to further a universal purpose—fighting for an idea, as they call it. Why was the Crusader braver than the pirate? Because he fought,

not for himself, but for the Cross. What force was it that met him with a valor as reckless as his own? The force of men who fought, not for themselves but for Islam. . . . Every idea for which Man will dies will be a Catholic idea. When the Spaniard learns at last that he is no better than the Saracen, and his prophet no better than Mahomet, he will arise, more Catholic than ever, and die on a barricade across the filthy slum he starves in, for universal liberty and equality.

To anyone familiar with only the early Shaw, this would seem like a very peculiar line for Juan to be taking. The term "idea" in this speech corresponds to an heroic ideal in *The Quintessence of Ibsenism*—a "universal purpose" or goal exemplified by the Cross, Islam, liberty, equality, and so forth. My initial discussion of the *Quintessence* revealed that there are two basic kinds of idealism (the reactionary and the progressive) and that Shaw in 1891 was less interested in distinguishing between them than in rejecting both in favor of a pragmatic approach. Moreover, my preliminary discussion of *Man and Superman* has shown how Shaw strengthened his critique of the negative side of idealism by equating a refusal to outgrow it with a state of damnation. But in the passage just quoted, it becomes apparent that Shaw's critical view of the positive side of idealism, far from being similarly intensified, has been completely altered. For now he follows the lead of the *Wagnerite* in stressing the *difference* between heroic and conventional ideals, with Don Juan being as eager to defend the former as to condemn the latter. Thus when the Devil, responding to Juan's praise of man's willingness to die for a "Catholic idea," retorts that people "will never be at a loss for an excuse for killing one another," Juan does not embrace this seemingly Shavian observation, but explains that he is "not now defending the illusory forms the great ideas take." Rather, he is defending the view that man, "who in his own selfish affairs is a coward to the backbone, will fight for an idea like a hero." In short, we now have a moral distinction between heroic ideals ("great ideas") and the conventional ones ("illusory forms") that comprise the catalogue of condemnations at the end of Satan's "force of Death" speech. The difference between the two lies in the attitude of the person holding the ideal: the names are the same.

—Alfred Turco Jr., *Shaw's Moral Vision: The Self and Salvation* (Ithaca: Cornell University Press, 1976): pp. 155–157.

Plot Summary of
Major Barbara

Major Barbara is a play with three acts that Shaw completed in September of 1905. The first production of the play took place at the Royal Court Theatre in London in November of 1905. It was first published in 1907 in *John Bull's Other Island and Major Barbara: also How he Lied to Her Husband.* By this time, Shaw was confident of his literary abilities. Up until now, he had tried to make his plays commercially successful, but now he wrote to please himself.

Act I demonstrates Shaw's skill with exposition. The act takes place in the library of Lady Britomart's London home after dinner on an evening in January 1906. Lady Britomart has summoned her son Stephen to come to the library so she can discuss his future. She asks that Stephen advise her on his plans, but really Lady Britomart is about to inform Stephen what his future should be. Lady Britomart also wants to discuss the futures of her two daughters. She has found a match for her daughter Sarah in Charles Lomax, but he will not come into his money for 10 years. In the meantime she must find a way to get an extra £800 a year for Sarah. Her daughter Barbara, she explains, presents a different sort of dilemma, because Barbara has decided on the Salvation Army over riches and career. Her likely mate, Adolphus Cusins, meets Lady Britomart's approval as a future husband, but as a Greek scholar he will generate no respectable income. Lady Britomart estimates that she must find £2000 a year for Barbara. She has been further occupied in finding Stephen a suitable mate.

Lady Britomart reminds her son that his father, Andrew Undershaft, is "rolling in money," but since the two have separated, she hardly considers asking her estranged husband for money. Stephen is uncomfortable at the mention of his father and his millions, because his fortune comes from cannons and other weapons of destruction. Stephen's mother clarifies that the business was not the cause of their separation:

> LADY BRITOMART: . . . He is always breaking the law. He broke the law when he was born: his parents were not married.
> STEPHEN: Mother! Is that true?
> LADY BRITOMART: Of course it's true: that was why we separated.
> STEPHEN: He married without letting you know this!

LADY BRITOMART: Oh no. To do Andrew justice, that was not the sort of thing he did. Besides you know the Undershaft motto: Unashamed. Everybody knew.

STEPHEN: But you said that was why you separated.

LADY BRITOMART: Yes, because he was not content with being a foundling himself: he wanted to disinherit you for another foundling. That was what I couldn't stand.

Lady Britomart continues to surprise and confuse her son with her revelations. Stephen declares that they cannot accept money from such a father, but his mother explains that they live on his father's income. To make matters worse for Stephen, Lady Britomart tells him that his father has been invited to visit and will arrive shortly.

At the same time, Barbara and Sarah come into the library with their beaus, Adolphus and Charles. The four young people arrive in good spirits. It is clear that Lady Britomart is used to running their lives as well. She announces the pending arrival of their father. Their conversation illustrates their personalities: Barbara, looking forward to her father's visit since he is another soul to convert; Sarah not thinking about much of anything; Lomax stuck in the jargon of the day; and Cusins acting like the scholar he is.

When Mr. Undershaft arrives, he treats Lady Britomart as if he never left. She does not respond in kind. The scene is filled with comedy, for he cannot recognize his own children, and he confuses Lomax with his son Stephen. He is grateful when Cusins clears up the confusion. As the conversation, difficult and tense at first, proceeds, Mr. Undershaft comments that the Salvation Army interests him. Barbara invites him to come to the West Ham shelter so that he can see her work up close.

But this invitation provokes a discussion of the morality of Mr. Undershaft's profession as a maker of cannons. Undershaft proposes to Barbara that if he visits the Army shelter, she should visit his cannon factory. The others join the plan and go to the drawing room so Barbara can conduct a service, leaving Lady Britomart and Stephen. He tries to convince her that their sudden attention toward their father is nothing of consequence:

STEPHEN: He has not stolen our affection from you. It is only curiosity.

LADY BRITOMART: I wont be consoled, Stephen.

The scene closes as she heads for the drawing room.

The West Ham chapter of the Salvation Army, a day later, is the setting for **Act II**. Again, someone has just finished a meal when the scene opens. A man, Snobby Price, and a woman, Rummy Mitchens, talk over a table. Perhaps echoing Shaw's views on capitalism, Snobby explains that though unemployed, he is an intelligent painter:

> [Y]es: intelligent beyond the station o life into which it has pleased the capitalists to call me; and they dont like a man that sees through em. Second, an intelligent bein needs a doo share of appiness; so I drink somethink cruel when I get the chawnce. Third, I stand by my class and do as little as I can so's to leave arf the job for me fellow workers. Fourth, I'm fly enough to know wots inside the law and wots outside it; and inside it I do as the capitalists do: pinch wot I can lay me ands on. . . . Wots the consequence? When trade is bad—and it's rotten bad just now—and the employers az to sack arf their men, they generally start on me.

Rummy makes it clear that she is only doing the workers at the Salvation Army a favor by letting them save her. Snobby is willing to be saved as well if he can get a free meal.

As they talk, Jenny Hill, a young Salvation Army worker, brings in an older man who seems hungry and down on his luck. Peter Shirley has lost his job because he looks older than he is. A proud man used to working for his income, he is reluctant at first but finally welcomes the offer of a meal. A rough-looking young man named Bill Walker comes in. His very pronounced accent emphasizes his rough exterior as he speaks first to Jenny: "Aw knaow you. Youre the one that took awy maw girl. Youre the one that set er agen me." His harsh tone soon changes into physical abuse and the others present try to step in to help Jenny. Bill continues to brutalize the group with menacing words until Shirley starts to taunt his manhood. Shirley suggests that Bill fight a man, instead of women and old people, and tells Bill of a wrestler named Todger Fairmile who would give him a fair fight. As the two continue to exchange insults, Major Barbara comes in.

She wants each to tell his own story. She starts with Peter Shirley and assures him that a steady man like him will always find work with God's help. When Major Barbara addresses Bill Walker, he goes on the defensive. Barbara pries out the name of his girl friend, who turns out to be another Salvation Army worker at their barracks. Barbara happily reports to Bill that another convert named Todger Fairmile, now a Sergeant in the Salvation Army, has saved his girl friend. She encourages Bill to meet Todger:

BARBARA: Go and talk to him, Bill. He'll convert you.
SHIRLEY: He'll convert your head into a mashed potato.
BILL: Aw aint afride of im. Aw aint afride of ennybody.

Their conversation continues when Mr. Undershaft arrives.

Barbara first introduces him to Peter Shirley, thinking that they both are what she has called Secularists. But her father corrects her: "My religion? Well, my dear, I am a Millionaire. That is my religion." This does not deter Barbara from talking more about her work to her father. When Mr. Undershaft notices the brooding Bill Walker, Barbara affirms her confidence that Bill will soon be converted away from the devil. Bill and Major Barbara exchange remarks, but she confidently assures him that conversion will make a man of him. Adolphus Cusins arrives and Major Barbara introduces him as her "bloke" to Bill. Walker sympathizes with Cusins but they continue to discuss Todger and his eventual conversion to better ways. Bill insists on advising Cusins to control Barbara before it is too late: "You tike may tip, mite. Stop er jawr; or youll doy afoah your tawm. Wore aht: thets wot youll be: wore aht."

Barbara notices her father again and asks Cusins to take over the tour of the shelter because she cannot spare more time from her work. This gives the two men an opportunity to exchange views and to get to know each other better. Undershaft recognizes that Cusins has only accepted the Salvation Army to be closer to his daughter. Quoting Euripides, Cusins explains that Barbara represents a happy life and loveliness to him. When pushed even further by Undershaft, Cusins affirms:

> I am in many ways a weak, timid, ineffectual person; and my health is far from satisfactory. But whenever I feel that I must have anything, I get it, sooner or later. I feel that way about Barbara. I dont like marriage: I feel intensely afraid of it; and I dont know what I shall do with Barbara or what she will do with me. But I feel that I and nobody else must marry her.

Though they have different views, the two agree that religion is the way for both of them to keep Barbara in their lives. When challenged about his beliefs, Mr. Undershaft makes it clear that he understands what true love and religious fervor are, but he says: "My friend: I never ask for what I can buy." His intention is to buy the Salvation Army to keep Barbara close.

When the others return, the conversation changes to the difficulties that the harsh winter has presented for the shelter and the Army in general. There is not enough money to carry on Barbara's work. When Mr. Undershaft offers her money, Barbara calls it blood money. She and Jenny agree that prayer and their planned march will help raise the needed funds. Then Bill Walker returns from his unsuccessful confrontation with Todger Fairmile. Barbara and Jenny feel bad that Bill suffered a beating, but Bill wants none of their sympathy. He offers to donate a pound so that they will leave him in peace. Mr. Undershaft offers to add another ninety-nine, contending that £100 would help the shelter a great deal. But Major Barbara does not want to be bought.

Mrs. Baines arrives. She is a Salvation Army worker who plans to help Major Barbara with the afternoon rally. She explains that a rich gentleman has offered £5000 to the Army if they can find another five men to match his figure. When she tells the group the man's name, Mr. Undershaft discloses that the name is a cover for Bodger, the whisky man. Mr. Undershaft also offers to match the sum. Mrs. Baines is understandably excited by his offer, but Barbara will have none of it. She does not want their money; she wants their souls. The others concentrate instead on the day's rally. Mr. Undershaft grabs their attention by volunteering to play the trombone. They all are set for the rally, but Barbara's attitude interrupts their excitement. In desperation, Barbara removes the Salvation Army badge from her coat and gives it to her father. She refuses to join them. As the others leave for the meeting, Barbara sinks down at the table. Bill Walker taunts her about the price of salvation. A dejected Barbara is left in Shirley's company as the scene ends.

In **Act III,** Lady Britomart goes the next day to write in the library after lunch. Charles, in his usual bumbling manner, cannot help but comment on Barbara's change of dress. (She is dressed in ordinary, fashionable clothes, instead of the Salvation Army uniform.) As he gets scolded yet again by Lady Britomart, Cusins comes in to tell of his night drinking with Mr. Undershaft. Although all present are amazed at his state, Barbara would rather hear about the Salvation Army meeting. Cusins recounts the great success in conversions and Mr. Undershaft's anonymous donation. Lady Britomart tells Adolphus he should leave the Army now that Barbara is no longer a part of it. Barbara asks Cusins if he was ever serious about the Army. As Cusins uncomfortably tries to answer, the butler announces Mr. Undershaft's arrival.

The younger people leave the room to get ready for their outing to the cannon works. Lady Britomart insists on talking with her husband about Stephen's taking over the business. Mr. Undershaft reiterates that a foundling must continue the Undershaft tradition. He tells her: "If you want to keep the foundry in the family, you had better find an eligible foundling and marry him to Barbara."

Stephen joins them. He tells his father that he has no desire to join the family business; he seeks instead a career in politics. At his mother's objections, Stephen stands up to her while his father supports his son's efforts at independence. But the two men argue over the government and national pride. When the others return, they all begin to talk of the cannon works. Mr. Undershaft explains his hands-off policy of management, which has resulted in great profits. When he tries to speak to Barbara, she replies angrily:

> Do you think I can be happy in this vulgar silly dress? I! who have worn the uniform. Do you understand what you have done to me? Yesterday I had a man's soul in my hand. I set him in the way of life with his face to salvation. But when we took your money he turned back to drunkenness and derision. I will never forgive you that.

But her father makes Barbara realize that her efforts were not in vain. She lights up at this thought and now looks forward to the factory visit. They all head off to the country.

Once at the factory town, all marvel at how clean and perfect everything is. Mr. Undershaft has found Peter Shirley a job and the workers speak highly of their employer. He joins the others and happily announces that his aerial artillery worked well in a Japanese victory. Cusins is upset, but the general attention changes to Lomax's careless use of a match near an explosives shed.

Lady Britomart's arrival from town interrupts them. She complains to Undershaft that he has unfairly kept all the wealth of the town to himself. When he clarifies that everything belongs to the Undershaft inheritance, Lady Britomart corrects him: " . . . all that plate and linen, all that furniture and those houses and orchards and gardens belong to us. They belong to me: they are not a man's business. I wont give them up." She no longer insists that Stephen inherit the business; instead, Lady Britomart wants Adolphus to marry Barbara and take over the company. When Undershaft reminds her of the stipulation that a foundling inherit, Cusins interjects that he has a confession to make. He has deceived Barbara not only about his work for the Army but also about his birth. Adolphus explains that his parents' marriage is not legal in England, since his mother is his father's deceased wife's sister.

Undershaft agrees that this would satisfy the stipulation, so the two begin to negotiate Cusins' salary. They finally agree, but Undershaft reminds Cusins of his new duty: "To give arms to all men who offer an honest price for them, without respect of persons or principles. . . ." Cusins believes he is above the money that has made Undershaft its slave. But Barbara laments the loss of their souls instead. Undershaft declares that he has saved her soul from the seven deadly sins:

> Food, clothing, firing, rent, taxes, respectability and children. Nothing can lift those seven millstones from Man's neck but money; and the spirit cannot soar until the millstones are lifted. I lifted them from your spirit. I enabled Barbara to become Major Barbara; and I saved her from the crime of poverty.

Cusins, Barbara, and Undershaft debate further. Undershaft maintains that voting only changes the names in a government while arms pull down governments and establish new orders. Cusins reluctantly agrees to this logic.

His future father-in-law pushes Cusins to make a choice. Undershaft suggests that they all leave Barbara and Adolphus alone to talk. As it progresses, their conversation focuses on power rather than money. Barbara seeks a higher power, but Cusins admits that her father's challenge to take over the business has won him over. Barbara believes finally that she must accept both Cusins and her father's offer of the inheritance. She now sees that the factory town "is where salvation is really wanted." Barbara's spirit is renewed at her realization. They rejoin the others and talk of starting a new life in the factory town as the play ends.

Major Barbara is often viewed as being mainly a commentary on weapons and power. However, Shaw always emphasizes his characters more than any political comment he might hope to make. Barbara is one of his strongest female characters, a woman of commitment and kindness, who needs only to grow up before she can achieve a meaningful union with her mate. As in *Man and Superman*, the play affirms marriage as both a happy ending and a fruitful beginning. ❀

List of Characters in
Major Barbara

Lady Britomart Undershaft is a lady of breeding and class, yet she can be outspoken and scolding. Lady Britomart has a very practical outlook on life and wants to secure the financial future of her children. She and her husband, Andrew Undershaft, have lived apart for much of her three children's lives, a situation Lady Britomart wishes to continue.

The only son of Lady Britomart and Andrew Undershaft, **Stephen Undershaft** takes life quite seriously for a young man. For the most part, he has lived attached to his mother and answers to all her whims. Lady Britomart plans for Stephen to take over the family business, a goal that Stephen does not share.

The older of the two Undershaft daughters, **Barbara** is not only a member of the Salvation Army but has reached the rank of Major due to her hard work and exceptional zeal. Despite or because of her family's wealth, Major Barbara considers it her duty in life to come to the aid of the less fortunate by bringing them into the family of God.

Sarah Undershaft is a more bored and mundane version of her older sister. Sarah prefers to tease her beau, Charles Lomax, and usually allows Barbara to deal with the more serious issues of life while Sarah pays attention to her looks and clothes.

Charles Lomax is a light-headed, young man of society who misuses contemporary social speech (to Lady Britomart's dismay). Charles is set on not taking life too seriously and marrying Sarah in the meantime. Charles, whom Sarah nicknames Cholly, tags along through most of the play and makes half-witted observations as he goes.

The serious and very devoted beau of Barbara, **Adolphus Cusins**, has embraced the Salvation Army expressly to be near her, although his zealous work on the Army's behalf does not betray his motive in any way. He is well read and intelligent, although somewhat belligerent in character when it comes to presenting and defending his own ideas. According to Mr. Undershaft, Cusins is a most suitable successor in the family business if only he met the unusual demands of the company's charter.

Andrew Undershaft, the long-absent father of the family, is a highly successful and single-minded business man who at first blush considers money and business above all else. The promised visit by his family to Undershaft's company town soon proves him to be a more complex and thoughtful man. Undershaft accepts his daughter Barbara's challenge to witness the work of the Salvation Army but his offer to contribute a large sum of money forces Barbara to quit the Army and the work to which she has dedicated so much energy.

Jenny Hill is Major Barbara's energetic and devoted Salvation Army assistant. Jenny works tirelessly for the sake of the Army and Barbara's goals. She even suffers physical assault at the hands of Bill Walker, all in the line of duty to the Army.

A middle-aged man recently out of work, **Peter Shirley** reluctantly accepts the offer of food at the Salvation Army shelter.

A young brutal man, **Bill Walker**, threatens and hits Jenny Hill. When Major Barbara confronts him and tells him of the power of God, Bill understandably does not believe her. Barbara challenges Bill to meet with Sergeant Todger Fairmile, a former wrestling champion now a convert to the ways of the Army, so that Bill can learn how to chose the right course in life. When Bill eventually returns, beaten and shamed by Todger, his resentful comments to Major Barbara undermine her own faith. ✸

Critical Views on
Major Barbara

[In this letter to Gilbert Murray, with whom Shaw consulted while writing the play, the playwright explains the process of rewriting as a response to Murray's comments on Act III of *Major Barbara*. Shaw concentrates on his reworking of Cusins and offers a clarification of Undershaft's character.]

To GILBERT MURRAY

Edstaston. Wem. Shropshire
7th October 1905

Dear Murray

Thanks for the Barbara stuff. If anything further occurs to you, send it along.

I want to get Cusins beyond the point of wanting power. I shall use your passage to bring out the point that Undershaft is a fly on the wheel; but Cusins would not make the mistake of imagining that he could be anything else. The fascination that draws him is the fascination of reality, or rather—for it is hardly a fascination—the impossiblility of refusing to put his hand to Undershaft's plough, which is at all events doing something, when the alternative is to hold aloof in a superior attitude and beat the air with words. To use your metaphor of getting his hand on the lever, his choice lies, not between going with Undershaft or not going with him, but between standing on the footplate at work, and merely sitting in a first class carriage reading Ruskin & explaining what a low dog the driver is and how steam is ruining the country.

I am writing the whole scene over again. The moisture which serves for air in Ireland spoiled it hopelessly. I will send the new version to you when it is in shape.

I have taken rather special care to make Cusins the reverse in every point of the theatrical strong man. I want him to go on his quality wholly, and not to make the smallest show of physical robustness or brute determination. His selection by Undershaft should be a puzzle to people who believe in the strong-silent-still-waters-run-deep hero of melodrama. The very name Adolphus Cusins is selected to that end.

As to the triumph of Undershaft, that is inevitable because I am in the mind that Undershaft is in the right, and that Barbara and Adolphus, with a great deal of his natural insight and cleverness, are very young, very romantic, very academic, very ignorant of the world. I think it would be unnatural if they were able to cope with him. Cusins averts discomfiture & scores off him by wit & humorous dexterity; but the facts are too much for him; and his strength lies in the fact that he, like Barbara, refuses the Impossibilist position (which their circumstances make particularly easy for them) even when the alternative is the most sensationally anti-moral department of commerce. The moral is drawn by Lomax "There is a certain amount of tosh about this notion of wickedness."

I have been writing this letter in scraps for three days—impossible to write letters here. I shall be back in London on Friday at latest.

Handsome of me not to make you a Rhodes scholar, by the way.

GBS

—George Bernard Shaw, Letter to Gilbert Murray, 7 October, 1905, in *Bernard Shaw: Collected Letters 1898–1910*, ed. Dan H. Laurence (New York: Viking, 1985): pp. 565–566.

⊛

MARTIN MEISEL ON POLITICS AND *MAJOR BARBARA*

[Martin Meisel, author of *Shaw and the Nineteenth-Century Theater* and *Realizations: Narrative, Pictorial, and Theatrical Arts of the Nineteenth Century*, is Professor of English and Comparative Literature at Columbia University. In this essay, Meisel examines the political elements in Shaw's plays, proposing that revolution represents transformation in *Major Barbara*.]

The prospect of apocalyptic revolutionary violence as an answer to inclusive institutionalized disorder becomes explicit in the plays for the first time in *Major Barbara*. *Major Barbara* begins where the Unpleasant Plays left off—with a demonstration of complicity as young Stephen learns the source, in Undershaft's Death and Destruction factory, of the good things he has taken for granted in his mother's house. This motif, slight and comic in the opening, becomes central and tragic in the body of the play as Barbara suffers Undershaft's demonstration of the grotesque complicity between religion and active charity on the one hand and the profitable manufacture of whisky and weaponry on the other. Barbara, like her audience-surrogate predecessors, is "beggared"—robbed of spiritual assurance and ethical object, of a vocation. But the play does not end with Barbara at this painful point; the dialectic continues, and the unstated third alternative of the earlier plays is now stated.

The end of the play, where Barbara finds her vocation again through Cusins and Undershaft, points directly to revolution not as the piecemeal achievement of a permeated socialist parliament nor even as the last stage of the erosion of private property, but as the only avenue of transformation. It is dominated by Undershaft, who, in his role as Industrial Capitalism, is given his devilish due for creating a private model of state capitalism, organized and welfarized and prosperous enough to be nearly revolution proof. But Undershaft, who has made the best of his chances in the present order, is by no means committed to its permanence or desirability; and he tempts Cusins, now the focus of action, with catastrophist propositions. These are *dramatically* validated in that the new audience-surrogate, poet, classical scholar, and lover, delicate of health and archetypal man of peace, finds he must assent to them in spite of himself. Undershaft proclaims the folly of a world that "won't scrap its old prejudices and its old moralities and its old religions and its old political constitutions"—hardly an evolutionist point of view. He declares that killing is "the only lever strong enough to overturn a social system." "Whatever can blow men up can blow society up. The history of the world is the history of those who had courage enough to embrace this truth." He dares Cusins to "make war on war." This is the challenge that "beats" Cusins, who reveals his desire to arm the common man with "a democratic power strong enough to force the intellectual oligarchy to use its genius for the general good or else perish." Cusins ultimately yields to the temptation of Undershaft—who has shown him the kingdoms of the world—because it appears, in his own questioning phrase, that "the way of life lies through the factory of death." "Yes," Barbara declares; "through the raising of hell to heaven and of man to God, through the unveiling of an eternal light in the Valley of The Shadow."

> —Martin Meisel, "Shaw and Revolution: The Politics of the Plays," in *Shaw: Seven Critical Essays,* ed. Norman Rosenblood (Toronto: University of Toronto Press, 1971): pp. 123–125.

⟨℘⟩

ROBERT COSKREN ON WAGNER'S INFLUENCE ON SHAW

[Robert Coskren has published articles on composer Richard Wagner and playwright George Bernard Shaw. In this essay, Coskren compares the major figures in Wagner's *Siegfried* to characters in *Major Barbara*. He proposes similarities between Wotan and Undershaft but maintains that Shaw's character "retains a strength which is all his own."]

That Shaw himself considered Undershaft impotent in precisely the manner of Wotan is more than evident in the parallels between the great laments provided the respective god figures. In one of the great set pieces of *Die Walküre,* and in a bitter utterance which is at the center of the *Ring* allegory, Wotan had narrated as an inexorable chain of past evils his stymied present: "When young love vanished, with its delights, my spirit aspired to power, and spurred by former wishes, I went and won myself the world. I thought no falsehood, yet I did falsely, carried out contracts where harm lay hid." This dark confession returns in Undershaft's own moving admission of an unsavory past; his "*tone dropping into one of bitter and brooding remembrance,*" he recalls: "I was an east ender. I moralized and starved until one day I swore that I would be a full fed man at all costs; that nothing should stop me except a bullet, neither reason nor morals nor the lives of other men. I said 'Thou shalt starve ere I starve'; and with that word I became free and great." Like Wotan, Undershaft has linked vital aspiration to past evils, and is to an extent still bound by them. Both are to be seen as "slaves" awaiting the arrival of the free man.

But such is the only real similarity between the two figures. For the rest, Shaw proceeds to demonstrate that even if Undershaft's power is qualified in the manner of Wotan, yet its extent is far greater than that of Wagner's god and infinitely more assured; this a development in keeping with the evolution of Wotan as depicted in *The Perfect Wagnerite*. In short, Undershaft/Wotan has achieved a coalition with Alberich: the capitalist has become ruler, the ruler capitalist. This alteration is symbolized in Perivale St Andrews, whose features are drawn to suggest simultaneously the Niebelheim of the dwarf and the shining home of the gods.

The Valhalla pedigree of Undershaft's foundry town is evident enough. As Wotan's domain assumes the form of "a castle with glittering pinnacles, which stands on a cliff in the background," so Perivale St Andrews is shaped according to a similar ideal: situated "*between hills*," it is "*an almost smokeless town of white walls, roofs of narrow green slates and red tiles, tall trees, domes. . . . beautifully situated and beautiful in itself. . . .*"

It is, however, as a structural alteration unimagined by Wagner that the home of Shaw's twentieth-century god should acquire the lineaments of a renovated Niebelheim as well. Its renovation at the hands of the modern Alberich in Undershaft (Shaw had remarked in *The Perfect Wagnerite* that Alberich "had found that Niebelheim was a very gloomy place") is hinted at in an exchange between Barbara and her father. Barbara, still in the nineteenth century, believes melodramatically that the workplace of the capitalist-industrialist must inevitably assume the sleazy character of the home of Wagner's dwarf. "I have always thought," she admits, "of it as a sort of pit where lost creatures with blackened faces stirred up smoking fires and were driven and tormented by my father." To this, "*scandalized,*" the enlightened Alberich in Undershaft can only reply, "My dear! it is a spotlessly clean and beautiful hillside town."

It is noteworthy, then that if Wotan and Undershaft share a fundamental impotence, Undershaft retains a strength which is all his own. His is the potency born of political realism and of the command of an economic punch to which Wagner's doomed god has no access. And for this reason the hero which Shaw's Wotan seeks represents a type worlds away from that of the young rabble rouser of Wagnerian fame: not an anarchist who will destroy Valhalla, but a capable ruler who will sustain it. As *Major Barbara* concludes, the role of the new Siegfried falls to Cusins. In the meantime he is put through a strict apprenticeship under the Wotan in Undershaft and the Brunnhild in Barbara. His lesson?—that which for Shaw is utterly requisite for the enlightened Siegfried: he is "to learn Alberic's trade and shoulder Alberic's burden."

—Robert Coskren, "*Siegfried* Elements in the Plays of Bernard Shaw," in *SHAW: The Annual of Bernard Shaw Studies, Volume Two,* ed. Stanley Weintraub, (University Park, PA: Pennsylvania State University Press, 1982): pp. 34–35.

(𝕤)

DIANE LONG HOEVELER ON THE SPIRITUALITY OF BARBARA AND CUSINS

[Diane Long Hoeveler, a professor of English at the University of Louisville, is the author of *Romantic Androgyny: The Women Within.* In this article, she compares the spirituality of Barbara and Cusins in *Major Barbara,* proposing that the two complement each other in their religious formation and evolution.]

Shaw presents his belief in spiritual evolution in Barbara, the embodiment of traditional Christianity, although her religious beliefs contain a strong degree of spiritual Lamarckianism. In Act I Barbara's original Christianity allows her to remark, "There are neither good men nor scoundrels: there are just children of one Father. . . . Theyre all just the same sort of sinner; and theres the same salvation ready for them all." Blake's aphorism "One law for the lion and the ox is oppression" comes to mind, and this truth must be embraced before Barbara can gain the spiritual wisdom she evidences in Act III. But even before that final scene, Barbara reveals a spiritual sophistication in her wooing of Bill Walker's soul. She wants to save him, not only for heaven, but for happiness and productivity in this world. She exhorts him to "Come with us, Bill. To brave manhood on earth and eternal glory in heaven."

If Barbara is spirit and love, Cusins is her complement, embodying the intellect and will. He has been traditionally viewed as a sort of synthesis of Barbara's idealism and Undershaft's realism. But Cusins is not simply a synthesis; rather, he is the spiritual complement of Barbara, the true son of and heir to the godhead. With appropriate irony, when Undershaft first meets his family he mistakes Cusins for his son. Indeed, Cusins and Undershaft have much in common, particularly their tolerant attitude toward the relative merits of all systems of belief. Just as Undershaft believes in money and gunpowder yet tells Barbara that he is a mystic, so does Cusins confess that he is "a collector of religions; and the curious thing is that I find I can believe them all." He further admits to Undershaft that he participates in the Salvation Army because he sees it as "the true worship of Dionysos."

Cusin's religion, like Barbara's, embraces the divinity that is inherent in humanity. Cusins describes his love for Barbara in religious terms: "Dionysos and all the others are in herself. I adored what was divine in her." Barbara and Cusins also share a religion that is an amalgamation of several systems of belief. Cusins tries to explain this to Undershaft when he remarks that, "The power Barbara wields her—the power that wields Barbara herself—is not Calvinism, not Presbyterianism, not Methodism. . . . Barbara is quite original in her religion." Because Undershaft has been able to recognize this quality in his daughter, he has decided on Barbara as his heir: "I shall hand on my torch to my daughter. She shall make my converts and preach my gospel. . . . money and gunpowder. Freedom and power. Command of life and command of death." But Barbara is incomplete in herself; she needs a consort and Cusins fulfills that role by "renouncing" his birth and becoming Undershaft's "son" and heir and Barbara's husband.

—Diane Long Hoeveler, "Shaw's Vision of God in *Major Barbara*," *The Independent Shavian* 17, no. 1–2 (double issue, 1978–1979): p. 17.

SIDNEY P. ALBERT ON SHAW AND THE LORD'S PRAYER

[Sidney P. Albert, Professor Emeritus of Philosophy at California State University, is the author of significant essays on *Major Barbara*. In this study, Professor Albert closely examines the Lord's Prayer and its resonances in Shaw's play. In particular, this extract uses the phrase "Our Father Which Art in Heaven" to expand on the father theme that Albert sees in the text.]

The father theme pervades *Major Barbara*. (The word "father" in one way or another, appears thirty times in Act I, and over half as often in each of the other two acts.) The first act is organized around the homecoming of the long absent father of the Undershaft family, Andrew Undershaft. The extended expository conversation between his wife, Lady Britomart, and their son, Stephen, insistently focuses anticipatory interest on this paterfamilias, who is constantly referred to and addressed as "father" throughout the play. In rapid order we learn of his enormous wealth, formidable worldly power, and essential immunity from accepted political and legal constraints. A munitious potentate whose ruling authority in his nearly three-centuries-old firm was conferred upon him in the manner of an Antonine emperor, he assumes superhuman dimensions virtually from the outset. When he does appear on the scene and is introduced to the family, the comic identity confusions that ensue, and his candid acknowledgment of the awkwardness of his position as stranger-father, testify at once to his paternal atypicality.

A deft and dramatic transition from the human to the divine plane is effected when Lady Britomart ascribes daughter Barbara's unconventional Salvation Army behavior to having come of age with "no father to advise her":

> BARBARA. Oh yes she has. There are no orphans in the Salvation Army.
> UNDERSHAFT. Your father there has a great many children and plenty of experience, eh?
> BARBARA [*looking at him with quick interest and nodding*] Just so. How did you come to understand that? [pp. 87–88]

Immediately thereafter comes his claim of even closer affinity to the Army:

> UNDERSHAFT. . . . I am rather interested in the Salvation Army. Its motto might be my own: Blood and Fire.
> LOMAX [*shocked*] But not your sort of blood and fire, you know.
> UNDERSHAFT. My sort of blood cleanses: my sort of fire purifies.

Conveyed is something more than the lethal efficacy of his weaponry: an enigmatic intimation of purgative powers drawn from control of the most vital and deadly forces of nature.

—Sidney P. Albert, "The Lord's Prayer and *Major Barbara*," in *SHAW: The Annual of Bernard Shaw Studies, Volume One*, ed. Charles A. Berst (University Park, PA: Pennsylvania State University Press, 1981): p. 111.

[Norman Gelber has also published on Robert Greene's *Orlando Furioso*. Here, Gelber examines the unequal social pairings in *Major Barbara*, specifically the marriage of Lady Britomart to Andrew Undershaft and the consequences that the marriage has on other characters in the work.]

Lady Britomart's superior attitude toward Mr. Undershaft, based on her descent from the Earl of Stevenage, introduces in the plot the factor of class difference as a key to the marital discord. She explains to Stephen that she separated from Undershaft because she could not tolerate his outlandish intention of disregarding their son's rightful inheritance: "He wanted to disinherit you for another foundling. That was what I couldn't stand." However, a closer examination of the inheritance issue also indicates that it involves her aristocratic background; she upholds the custom of primogeniture because the inherited wealth would complement the prestigious status which her rank confers on Stephen. And in view of her admission that she stooped to marry Undershaft because of his wealth, it is reasonable to assume that she desires her son to have a better opportunity to marry a woman of his own class rather than one of the newly rich.

Although the inheritance issue constitutes the principle factors in Lady Britomart's decision to separate from her husband, it is by no means the only divisive element in this unstable marriage. There are also sharp differences in social origins, in social manners, and in moral standards that contribute to the couple's incompatibility. Lady Britomart's emphasis on her aristocratic lineage, together with her disparagement of her husband's plutocratic wealth, has already been noted. In fact, her stated condescension to marry a member of the newly rich has not diminished her pride as a member of the peerage; she assumes that her husband got the better of the "bargain."

Undershaft himself makes no attempt to hide his lowly origin. He has evidently informed Lady Britomart that he was an illegitimate foundling, and he acknowledges that he lacks the credentials of a gentleman and adequate schooling: "As you know, I am not a gentleman; and I was never educated." Elsewhere he admits that he has suffered poverty: "But I have been a common man and a poor man; and it has no romance for me." Despite his phenomenal climb from rags to riches, the fact that his wealth derives from the manufacture and sale of armaments—an occupation that the aristocracy held in low esteem—leads Lady Britomart to belittle him as a "vulgar tradesman."

Arising from the difference in social origins are the contrasting social manners of this misallied couple. Assuming the role of a fastidious aristocrat, Lady Britomart reproaches Undershaft for being sentimental, for addressing her familiarly as "Biddy," and for not wearing his necktie straight. Such scolding, administered at times in the company of the family, reflects her highborn disdain for his vulgar habits. Trivial or commonplace as these points of friction may seem, they do serve to reinforce the impression that the peeress and the tycoon are socially incompatible.

Finally, Lady Britomart and Undershaft stand poles apart in their attitude toward morality, and once again she considers herself the arbiter of what is right.

—Norman Gelber, "The 'Misalliance' Theme in *Major Barbara*," *The Shaw Review* 15, no. 2 (May 1972): pp. 67–68.

☙

DANIEL DERVIN ON DETERMINATION IN *MAJOR BARBARA*

[Daniel Dervin is the author of *Bernard Shaw: A Psychological Study* and *Matricentric Narratives: Recent British Women's Fiction in a Postmodern Mode*. Here, Dervin suggests that although love is at the heart of *Major Barbara*, Shaw concentrates more on portraying the determined will of Barbara and Andrew Undershaft.]

Major Barbara (1905) combines the power and "practical genius" of the munitions maker, the scholar's humanism and historical awareness, and Barbara's "love and faith" as she is converted from Christianity to the Life Force. Barbara is in fact the historical shift of the Life Force from an obsolete form of religion to the new one heralded by Shaw. And similarly Lavinia in *Androcles and the Lion* (1912) is converted from the "stories and dreams" of Christianity to the unknown religion of the future.

Barbara, Lavinia, and later on Joan are in the line of composed, idealistic, and strong-willed heroines whose original in the plays was

Vivie Warren. But because the center of Vivie's Capitalistic society cannot hold, lacking the cohesion of Vitalism, the characters are scattered at the end of *Mrs. Warren's Profession*. The movement in the Vitalist and Discussion Plays, however, is centripetal: new combinations form new wholes. And this operation of energy binding together ever larger units of society, this *élan vital*, is similar to Freud's object-libido which, when it is aim-inhibited as Shaw's mainly was, goes out to the world forming bonds with its subliminated energy. The object-instincts along with the self-preservative ego-instincts comprise the great creative and civilizing force in life that Freud later came to call Eros.

In tracing social combinations back to their sources in libidinal energies, we find ourselves in a better position to examine certain other implications of these plays. In *Major Barbara* there is a certain correlation between the three main characters and the instincts referred to above. Although Andrew Undershaft has been identified as a maker of money and gunpowder, the forces of death and destruction, it is not in that dimension alone which Shaw treats him:

> I was an east ender. I moralized and starved until one day I swore that I would be a full-fed man at all costs—that nothing should stop me except a bullet, neither reason nor morals nor the lives of other men. I said "Thou shalt starve ere I starve"; and with that word I became free and great. I was a dangerous man until I had my will: now I am a useful, beneficient, kindly person. (MB, p. 435)

He has survived and thrived because of his will to self-preservation and because of his capacity to deal with aggression, both of which are functions of the ego-instincts. But his great personal success, while paradoxically a potential boon for mankind, has left him impoverished in other ways. A foundling and a self-made man (another instance of gravitational rise), he has only a nominal wife and family, and no sustaining personal relationships. His life is his work. He is living self-preservation, industry, and externalized aggression, but not fully human; and therefore it becomes essential that he be united with the two libidinal object-instinct characters, Barbara and Cusins, in order to channel the power for evil into power for good and to form an integrated entity. This might be called the underlying Freudian synthesis toward which the play moves.

—Daniel Dervin, *Bernard Shaw: A Psychological Study* (Lewisburg: Bucknell University Press, 1975): pp. 275–276.

Plot Summary of
Pygmalion

Subtitled "A Romance in Five Acts," *Pygmalion* includes a preface and closing remarks. Shaw completed the play in June of 1912. It was originally published in a German translation, but the first publication in English appeared in the New York periodical *Everybody's Magazine* in November of 1914. The first English production of the play was presented at His Majesty's Theatre, London, on April 11, 1914. In *Pygmalion*, Shaw did not make the same effort to represent particular accents as he did in other plays (for example, Bill Walker in *Major Barbara*). Nevertheless, Shaw establishes the fact clearly and early on that Eliza Doolittle speaks with a most noticeable accent.

The play's title refers to the myth of the sculptor Pygmalion, who created and then fell in love with a beautiful statue. His love transformed the statue into a flesh and blood woman, Galatea. In Shaw's story, a language professor transforms a guttersnipe girl into a beautiful woman capable of posing as a duchess. Although Shaw insisted that his play was not intended to have romantic overtones, given his choice of title, viewers cannot be blamed for insisting that *Pygmalion* is actually a romance. Perhaps Shaw agreed subconsciously.

Act I opens on a summer evening in London. It is pouring rain and all about are trying to hail cabs. Two women in evening dress take shelter from the rain, Mrs. Eynsford-Hill and her daugher Clara. They are waiting for Freddy Eynsford-Hill, Clara's brother, to find them a cab. The mother is kinder in tone as the two talk about Freddy, but she still considers her son's efforts insufficient when he returns to report that there are no cabs to be found. Clara thinks her brother and life in general are tiresome. In the meantime, a flower girl, Eliza Doolittle, listens to their conversation. As Freddy goes off again in search of a cab, he bumps into Eliza and knocks over her flowers. Eliza addresses him by his first name, thus catching the attention of his mother and sister. A conversation of sorts among the women ensues. Clara is indignant that such a girl would dare speak to them, while her mother is willing to pay for the ruined flowers. Eliza only thinks of getting some money.

While trying to sell flowers to a gentleman, Eliza hears a bystander warn her that there is a man nearby "taking down every blessed word youre saying." Eliza, upset at this news, starts a racket among the crowd. As a person makes a comment or tries to calm Eliza, the note-taker interrupts the speaker to tell him something about his origin. The people in the crowd mistake the note-taker for a policeman. He correctly tells Mrs. Eynsford-Hill and her daughter where both were brought up. Exasperated at this, mother and daughter leave to find Freddy. A gentleman curiously asks the note-taker how he manages to identify people's origins.

> THE NOTE TAKER: Simply phonetics. The science of speech. Thats my profession: also my hobby. Happy is the man who can make a living by his hobby! You can spot an Irishman or a Yorkshireman by his brogue. *I* can place any man within six miles. I can place him within two miles in London. Sometimes within two streets.

The note-taker, quite proud of his abilities, explains further to the gentleman, using Eliza as his example:

> THE NOTE TAKER: You see this creature with her kerbstone English: the English that will keep her in the gutter to the end of her days. Well, sir, in three months I could pass that girl off as a duchess at an ambassador's garden party. I could even get her a place as lady's maid or shop assistant, which requires better English.

They chat some more, especially about Eliza's exaggerated accent. When the two men introduce themselves, they realize they are professional colleagues. The gentleman is Colonel Pickering, an expert in Indian dialects. Professor Henry Higgins is the confident note-taker. The two go off to Pickering's hotel to have supper and talk of their mutual interests.

Eliza, upset at being ignored so easily, turns her attention to Freddy, who has finally arrived with a cab. Eliza tells him his mother and sister have left. Full of herself and encouraged by the extra change she has managed to get from the crowd, Eliza chooses to take the cab home. The cab takes her to Angel Court, a poor and delapidated section of London. The taxi driver, enjoying the laugh he has had at Eliza's expense, decides not to charge her as the act ends.

The scene changes to Professor Higgins' home on the following morning in **Act II**. Higgins has spent the morning showing Colonel Pickering his laboratory and home on Wimpole Street. As they talk, Mrs. Pearce, the housekeeper, announces the arrival of a young woman:

> MRS. PEARCE: Well, sir, she says youll be glad to see her when you know what she's come about. She's quite a common girl, sir. Very common

indeed. I should have sent her away, only I thought perhaps you wanted her to talk into your machines. I hope I've not done wrong: but really you see such queer people sometimes.

Higgins thinks he can use the unexpected visit as an opportunity to show Pickering how he records accents on his phonograph. But when he recognizes Eliza, Higgins is no longer interested. Eliza tells him she has come for lessons. Pickering interrupts Higgins' insulting remarks to let Eliza explain:

> THE FLOWER GIRL: I want to be a lady in a flower shop stead of sellin at the corner of Tottenham Court Road. But they wont take me unless I can talk more genteel. He said he could teach me. Well, here I am ready to pay him—not asking any favor—and he treats me zif I was dirt.

She introduces herself to Pickering and Higgins. Finally, when Pickering turns the experiment into a bet, offering to pay for all expenses, Higgins considers the idea seriously, and decides to instruct Eliza. Quite enthusiastic about the venture, Higgins orders Mrs. Pearce to burn Eliza's clothes, get her new ones, and generally take charge of the young woman. Both Mrs. Pearce and Eliza react sharply to these orders: Eliza is insulted and Mrs. Pearce acts concerned about Higgins' extreme rudeness.

> MRS. PEARCE: . . . I want to know on what terms the girl is to be here. Is she to have any wages? And what is to become of her when youve finished your teaching? You must look ahead a little.
> HIGGINS: Whats to become of her if I leave her in the gutter? Tell me that, Mrs. Pearce.
> MRS. PEARCE: Thats her own business, not yours, Mr. Higgins.
> HIGGINS: Well, when Ive done with her, we can throw her back into the gutter; and then it will be her own business again; so thats all right.
> LIZA: Oh, youve no feeling heart in you: you dont care for nothing but yourself. Here! Ive had enough of this. I'm going. You ought to be ashamed of yourself, you ought.

Higgins tries to persuade Eliza with chocolates, but Pickering demands that Higgins be realistic and state the terms of the arrangement clearly, which he does:

> HIGGINS: . . . Eliza: you are to live here for the next six months, learning how to speak beautifully, like a lady in a florist's shop. If youre good and do whatever youre told, you shall sleep in a proper bedroom, and have lots to eat, and money to buy chocolates and take rides in taxis. If youre naughty and idle you will sleep in the back kitchen among the black beetles, and be walloped by Mrs. Pearce with a broomstick. At the end

of six months you shall go to Buckingham Palace in a carriage, beauti- fully dressed. If the King finds out youre not a lady, you will be taken by the police to the Tower of London, where your head will be cut off as a warning to other presumptuous flower girls. If you are not found out, you shall have a present of seven-and-sixpence to start life with as a lady in a shop. If you refuse this offer you will be a most ungrateful wicked girl: and the angels will weep for you. Now are you satisfied, Pickering? Can I put it more plainly and fairly, Mrs. Pearce?

Generally satisfied with Higgins' remarks, Mrs. Pearce takes Eliza to a third floor bedroom. There Mrs. Pearce scandalizes Eliza by telling her she must take a bath, a new and frightening prospect for the young woman. Eliza protests and screams as Mrs. Pearce starts to scrub her clean.

In the meantime, Pickering questions Higgins about his conduct where women are concerned. Once again, Higgins bluntly responds:

> HIGGINS: . . . I find that the moment I let a woman make friends with me, she becomes jealous, exacting, suspicious, and a damned nuisance. I find that the moment I let myself make friends with a woman, I be- come selfish and tyrannical. Women upset everything. When you let them into your life, you find that the woman is driving at one thing and youre driving at another.

Mrs. Pearce comes into the room with Eliza's hat, which she has promised not to discard. Higgins decides to keep it "as a curiosity." Mrs. Pearce finds it necessary to remind Professor Higgins that he should take more care about his behavior, his manners at table, and his tem- per now that such a particular young woman is living in the house. Higgins reluctantly agrees to this and Mrs. Pearce leaves the room.

She returns shortly to announce the arrival of a dustman, a man named Alfred Doolittle. He has come for his daughter. Higgins shouts at him and accuses Doolittle of extortion and blackmail. Doolittle tries to clarify that he has come to give Eliza the belongings she has re- quested. He explains that a young boy who accompanied Eliza to Wimpole Street passed on her request. Higgins tells Doolittle to take his daughter away. With Mrs. Pearce out of the room, Doolittle takes a different tack with Higgins:

> DOOLITTLE: . . . Well, the truth is, Ive taken a sort of fancy to you, Gov- ernor; and if you want the girl, I'm not so set on having her back home again but what I might be open to an arrangement. Regarded in the light of a young woman, she's a fine handsome girl. As a daughter she's

not worth her keep; and so I tell you straight. All I ask is my rights as a father; and youre the last man alive to expect me to let her go for nothing; for I can see youre one of the straight sort, Governor. Well, whats a five-pound note to you? and whats Eliza to me?

PICKERING: I think you ought to know, Doolittle, that Mr. Higgins' intentions are entirely honorable.

DOOLITTLE: Course they are, Governor. If I thought they wasn't, I'd ask fifty. . . .

PICKERING: Have you no morals, man?

DOOLITTLE: Cant afford them, Governor. Neither could you if you was as poor as me.

Doolittle's approach somehow appeals to Higgins. He wants to give him ten pounds, but Doolittle insists on the original five pounds. He promises to spend it on a "good spree."

As Doolittle is about to leave with his money, a young girl dressed in a Japanese kimono comes into the room. It is Eliza and her father exclaims when he recognizes her. Higgins threatens Eliza that her father will take her away. Eliza quickly contradicts Higgins: "Not him. You dont know my father. All he come here for was to touch you for some money to get drunk on." Doolittle leaves them and Mrs. Pearce has Eliza go off to try on her new dresses.

The scene changes to a lesson. Higgins has Eliza recite the alphabet. He screams at her when she mispronounces the first few letters. Pickering stands by to encourage Eliza. She is able, finally, to pronounce "c" in cup correctly. The men are encouraged. Higgins sends Eliza back to Mrs. Pearce as the act closes.

For **Act III,** the scene shifts to Mrs. Higgins' home. It is her "at-home" day when she receives guests for afternoon tea. Her son has come uninvited. She scolds him for doing so, saying: "You offend all my friends: they stop coming whenever they meet you." Higgins does not pay much attention to his mother's comments for he has come with the purpose of putting Eliza to a test.

HIGGINS: . . . Ive taught her to speak properly: and she has strict orders as to her behavior. She's to keep to two subjects: the weather and everybody's health—Fine day and How do you do, you know—and not to let herself go on to things in general. That will be safe.

MRS. HIGGINS: Safe! To talk about our health! about our insides! perhaps about our outsides! How could you be so silly, Henry?

HIGGINS: . . . Pickering is in it with me. Ive a sort of bet that I'll pass her off as a duchess in six months. I started on her some months ago. . . .

As Higgins proceeds with his explanation, the maid announces Mrs. Higgins' first guests: Mrs. Eynsford-Hill and her daughter Clara. Higgins does not recognize them at first. Then Colonel Pickering arrives followed by Freddy Eynsford-Hill. They chat until Eliza comes in. Beautifully dressed, she addresses the group with very precise pronunciation. Mrs. Higgins takes control of the conversation and introduces one of the two "safe" topics: the weather. Eliza delivers a sophisticated forecast to the amazement of all.

Then she changes the topic to health by stating that her aunt died of influenza. Eliza adds: "But it's my belief they done the old woman in." The guests are somewhat puzzled by some of Eliza's other colorful expressions. Freddy thinks Eliza and her speech are equally charming. He is sure that Eliza is using "the new small talk" quite well. Mrs. Higgins lets her guests think that Freddy is correct as she says good-bye to Eliza. Clara, normally bored by everything, remarks positively on Eliza's speech as well. Then the Eynsford-Hill ladies also leave.

When it is safe for them to talk openly, Higgins asks his mother's opinion. Mrs. Higgins concludes that his phonetic training and Eliza's dressmaker have made a great impression, but that Eliza will never learn proper language in her son's company. Nevertheless, neither Higgins nor Pickering can contain their enthusiasm over the experiment to turn Eliza "into a quite different human being by creating a new speech for her." Mrs. Higgins orders them to keep quiet. She points out that neither of them sees "the problem of what is to be done with her afterwards." Both men dismiss this as unimportant.

The scene shifts. It is a summer evening and Pickering, Higgins, and Eliza have arrived for a reception. Those attending are in evening dress. All is well until a former pupil of Professor Higgins named Nepommuck stops to talk with him. The whiskered man has become a famous interpreter and linguistic expert. When he leaves to assist a Greek diplomat, Pickering and Higgins wonder if Nepommuck will discover the truth about Eliza.

As the reception proceeds, the host and hostess are obviously impressed by Eliza. They are asking Higgins to tell them all about her, when Nepommuck interrupts to proclaim that Eliza is a fraud. He declares that she speaks too perfectly to be English; he believes that Eliza is Hungarian and of royal blood. The host and hostess accept his assessment. The act ends as Eliza talks to Pickering and Higgins:

> LIZA: I dont think I can bear much more. The people all stare so at me. An old lady has just told me that I speak exactly like Queen Victoria. I am sorry if I have lost your bet. I have done my best: but nothing can make me the same as these people.
> PICKERING: You have not lost it, my dear. You have won it ten times over.
> HIGGINS: Let us get out of this. I have had enough of chattering to these fools.

Act IV begins at midnight. Higgins and Pickering have returned to the Wimpole Street home to relax after an absorbing day and evening. Eliza delivers Higgins' slippers and then sits quietly to one side. Both men discuss the day's events without including Eliza in the conversation. Pickering congratulates Higgins for his triumph. Higgins complains that it has been "a purgatory" throughout. They leave to go to bed and Higgins asks for his slippers. Eliza picks them up and throws them at Higgins:

> HIGGINS: . . . Anything wrong?
> LIZA: Nothing wrong—with you. Ive won your bet for you, havnt I? Thats enough for you. *I* dont matter, I suppose.
> HIGGINS: You won my bet! You! Presumptuous insect! *I* won it. What did you throw those slippers at me for?
> LIZA: Because I wanted to smash your face. I'd like to kill you, you selfish brute. Why didnt you leave me where you picked me out of—in the gutter?

Higgins does not understand her reaction in the slightest. He maintains that she has never been ill-treated, she is only imagining things, and a good night's sleep will fix everything. Higgins tells Eliza not to worry because there are plenty of men to marry her:

> HIGGINS: I daresay my mother could find some chap or other who would do very well.
> LIZA: We were above that at the corner of Tottenham Court Road.
> HIGGINS: What do you mean?
> LIZA: I sold flowers. I didnt sell myself. Now youve made a lady of me I'm not fit to sell anything else. I wish youd left me where you found me.

The heated discussion between the two worsens. Eliza insists on knowing which of her things belong to her since, when she leaves, she does not want to be accused of stealing. Higgins loses his temper and slams out of the room.

The scene switches to the street outside. Eliza has changed her evening clothes. She finds Freddy waiting outside, where he explains he spends most of his evenings. Freddy declares his love and kisses Eliza. A policemen comes up to questions them. The couple walks away, kisses again, and once more is questioned by a policeman. When a taxi approaches, the very depressed Eliza decides they will spend the rest of the evening driving about. As the act ends, she plans to consult with Mrs. Higgins the next day.

In **Act V,** Mrs. Higgins is writing in her drawing room when the scene opens. Higgins and Pickering have arrived, and according to the maid, Higgins has called the police. When he sees his mother, he bursts out that Eliza is missing. (Mrs. Pearce informed Higgins that Eliza had collected her things early that morning and left.) Mrs. Higgins begins to scold both men for notifying the police. As she goes on, she is interrupted by her maid, who announces the arrival of a gentleman by the name of Doolittle to see Professor Higgins. Everyone is surprised to see that Doolittle, now dressed as a gentleman, has changed so much. Doolittle admits that he too is overwhelmed and uncomfortable because of his altered state. His new lot in life resulted from a comment made by Higgins to a wealthy American that Doolittle was "the most original moralist at present in England." Doolittle has inherited a yearly income from the American, provided that he lecture for a moral reform league. He clarifies:

> DOOLITTLE: It aint the lecturing I mind. I'll lecture them blue in the face. I will, and not turn a hair. It's making a gentleman of me that I object to. Who asked him to make a gentleman of me? I was happy. I was free. I touched pretty nigh everybody for money when I wanted it, same as I touched you, Enry Iggins.

Mrs. Higgins reacts favorably to Doolittle's new fortune because she believes he can now provide for Eliza's future.

But Higgins objects; he has paid five pounds for the girl. At that remark, Mrs. Higgins reveals that Eliza is upstairs. She tells her son to keep quiet and listen while she explains:

> MRS. HIGGINS: . . . She worked very hard for you, Henry. . . . Well, it seems that when the great day of trial came, and she did this wonderful thing for you without making a single mistake, you two sat there and never said a word to her, but talked together of how glad you were that it was all over and how you had been bored with the whole thing. And then you were surprised because she threw your slippers at you! I should have thrown the fire-irons at you.

Mrs. Higgins insists that if her son behaves she will summon Eliza so they all can get back on friendly terms. She asks Doolittle to step out so as not to shock his daughter.

When Eliza enters, she gracefully greets everyone. She addresses her remarks to Pickering, trying to ignore Higgins' insults. Eliza thanks the Colonel for helping her learn how real ladies and gentleman behave. Pickering hopes that Eliza will return to Wimpole Street and asks if she will forgive Higgins. When Doolittle reenters the room, Eliza lets out a howl. Higgins feels vindicated at her apparent relapse.

Eliza collects herself as her father tells them he has dressed up because it is his wedding day. He plans to marry Eliza's "stepmother" in true middle-class fashion. He invites Eliza and everyone to join him at the wedding. The others go to get ready for the event, leaving Eliza alone with Higgins.

> LIZA: You want me back only to pick up your slippers and put up with your tempers and fetch and carry for you.
> HIGGINS: I havnt said I wanted you back at all.
> LIZA: Oh, indeed. Then what are we talking about?
> HIGGINS: About you, not about me. If you come back I shall treat you just as I have always treated you. I cant change my nature; and I dont intend to change my manners. My manners are exactly the same as Colonel Pickering's.
> LIZA: Thats not true. He treats a flower girl as if she was a duchess.
> HIGGINS: And I treat a duchess as if she was a flower girl.

Their conversation continues in this vein. Higgins offers to adopt Eliza and provide an income for her. He also suggests she might marry Pickering, but then realizes that he and his friend are both confirmed bachelors. Higgins tells her to find some sentimental bore if she prefers a common life. Testing her independence, Eliza responds:

> LIZA: Oh, you are a cruel tyrant. I cant talk to you: you turn everything against me: I'm always in the wrong. But you know very well all the time that youre nothing but a bully. You know I cant go back to the gutter, as you call it, and that I have no real friends in the world but you and the Colonel. . . . But dont you be too sure that you have me under your feet to be trampled on and talked down. I'll marry Freddy, I will, as soon as I'm able to support him.

Higgins laughs at her prospect of marrying Freddy but recoils when she threatens to work for the translator Nepommuck. Eliza sees through his angry reaction and takes heart. She understands that she need not fear Higgins any more. As Eliza leaves with Mrs. Higgins for the church, she bids good-bye to Higgins and promises never to see him again. Ignoring this, he issues orders to her as usual as the play ends.

Despite the play's lack of a truly romantic ending, *Pygmalion* was successful on both sides of the Atlantic. Higgins' speeches are didactic and arrogant—and yet somehow viewers were enchanted. Shaw claimed that Henry Sweet, a cross and contentious real-life language expert, was his model for Henry Higgins, but critics could not help but see Shaw's own didactic opinions in Higgins' speeches, and they suspected that Shaw himself was the true Higgins. And just as Higgins does not possess the necessary qualities for a romance, Shaw could never quite pull off the romantic, happily-ever-after ending in his own life. When he titled this play, making reference to a great classical love story, perhaps subconsciously he was engaging in wishful thinking. ✿

List of Characters in
Pygmalion

In the opening scene, **Clara Eynsford-Hill**, a young woman of society, serves as a strong contrast to the simple and poor Eliza.

Mrs. Eynsford-Hill, the mother of Freddy and Clara, is obviously a lady of society.

Freddy Eynsford-Hill is a stereotypic upper class man of few intellectual recourses. In the opening scene Freddy is helpless in the rain, and in the meeting with a transformed Eliza he is hopelessly enamored.

Eliza Doolittle, the poor young woman who takes Higgins up on his promise to make her an upper class lady of distinction, evolves into an individual so cultured as to be unrecognizable to her own father. Eliza's remaking is a supposed victory for her mentor Higgins but represents an awakening for Eliza inside her renovated exterior.

Colonel Pickering, a renowned linguist, comes to London specifically to meet Higgins. Unexpectedly, they meet at the same time that Higgins first hears Eliza and her distinctive accent. Pickering is the gentleman that Higgins is not. The Colonel tempers the experiment by thinking of Eliza's welfare more than the promise of winning his challenge.

An arrogant, self-centered, and insensitive man, **Professor Henry Higgins** is a famous dialectician who issues a challenge to his professional colleague, Colonel Pickering—that of transforming Eliza from a "gutter snipe" into a lady fit for full participation in society. He puts Eliza through rigorous vocal and cultural training to reach his goal, while disregarding the personal needs of his pupil.

Higgins' housekeeper, **Mrs. Pearce**, watches over Eliza to assist in the more personal details of Eliza's evolution.

At the outset, the dust man **Alfred Doolittle** is a practical man who clearly acknowledges his lot in life. Later, however, because of a chance comment by Higgins, Doolittle becomes the unexpected heir to a fortune. Like Eliza, Doolittle experiences a radical change in destiny.

Mrs. Higgins, the Professor's mother, is resigned to the fact that her son has his limitations. She clearly supports Eliza during and after her training. Mrs. Higgins takes Eliza's side when her son ignores the personal repercussions of Eliza's transformation.

A former pupil of Higgins, **Nepommuck** certifies publicly that not only is Eliza a lady but that she is of noble birth. ✻

Critical Views on
Pygmalion

[In the summer of 1921, Shaw heard rumors that the rights to *Pygmalion* had been given by Siegfried Trebitsch for a musical rewriting of the work. Shaw is clearly against the idea. Here he explains to Trebitsch in very specific financial terms why he would not allow a *Pygmalion* operetta.]

To SIEGFRIED TREBITSCH

Herne Bay. [Kent]
28th August 1921

My dear Trebitsch

At the end of July I was at a Hydro (Wasserkur Anstalt—really a hotel) on the Yorkshire moors. Charlotte got ill and could not travel on the day we intended to leave; and I had to make up my mind to stay there with nothing to do for four or five days. So I set to work hard at Gitta, and nothing but Gitta, and finished her. That is to say, I finished my first draft of the dialogue in shorthand. I have not yet seen the typed transcript; and I have yet to revise that and to put in all the stage business; but still the main job is done; the rest is only drudgery and routine. I have not done justice to your poetry and your love of intense unhappiness, which convinces me that you have never really been unhappy in your life. Lenkheim, though a very correct professor, with all the proper feelings of an outraged husband, struck me as being rather a dull dog (like a real professor); and though I have not exactly made him a *mari à la mode*, I have ventured to make him a little less oppressively conventional than he would be in Austria, where they still fight duels (or at least think they ought to fight them) and do not admire Lenin & Trotsky as much as their late Apostolic Emperor. I have got a little mild fun out of Mrs Haldenstedt and left her really happy; and, though of course I havnt dared to say so, I have great hopes that the audience will feel pretty sure that in spite of Gitta's broken heart she will have at least a dozen other delightfully tragic affairs to amuse her before she finally retires as too old for adultery, and takes to religion with a spiritual adviser of thirty.

That is the good news. The bad is this Pygmalion business, of which I solemnly swear I never heard a word until Hamon wrote to me about Lehar. Your letter must have been lost in the post; for neglectful as I am of business I would never have let such a horrible disaster occur if I had known about it. Never again will I face the loss and disgrace the thrice accursed Chocolate Soldier brought upon me. Whilst its vogue lasted—even whilst the mere memory of its vogue lasted—Arms & The Man (Helden) was banished from the stage: nobody would touch it. Pygmalion is my most steady source of income: it saved me from ruin during the war, and still brings in a substantial penny every week. To allow a comic opera to supplant it is out of the question. I might possibly consider an offer of £10,000 English money; but as matters stand now, if they attempt to use a word of my dialogue, or to connect my name or my play in any way with their abominable opera I will let loose all the engines of the Copyright law to destroy them utterly. I have no choice in the matter: the manager [Charles Macdona] who is touring with the play in the provinces could sue me for damages if I ruined his business by letting Lehar loose on him. Therefore tell them anything you please; but stop them.

Did you realize that 5 per cent of the librettist's fees would mean 1/4 per cent at most, and possibly 1/8 per cent of the gross receipts? They could hardly afford to pay him more than 5%, and they would certainly do their best to make him accept 2 1/2% or less. At 2 1/2%, on a house of £100, he would get £2–10–0 and pay you two shillings & sixpence. An insane arrangement, especially as the rights of Pygmalion are worth far more than the original work of any librettist.

We must extricate ourselves from this somehow: a Pygmalion operetta is quite out of the question.

In haste, ever
G. Bernard Shaw

—George Bernard Shaw, Letter to Siegfried Trebitsch, 28 August 1921, in *Bernard Shaw: Collected Letters 1911–1925*, ed. Dan H. Laurence (New York: Viking, 1985): pp. 729–731.

[Jean Reynolds teaches writing and literature at Polk Community College in Florida. Here Reynolds applies Jacques Derrida's idea of *supplement* to the relationship she sees between Higgins and Eliza in *Pygmalion*. Reynolds contends, using both a negative and a positive interpretation of the Derridean term, that Shaw explores ambiguities in his text.]

In its negative aspect, a *supplement* is an inferior copy, a superfluous addition, or an afterthought. "Inferior" is how Higgins sees his pupil, and he rejects Eliza as a second-rate imitation of himself. When she tries to charm him in his mother's drawing room, he reprimands her: "Dont you dare try this game on me. I taught it to you; and it doesnt take me in" (767). To his mother, he says, "You will jolly soon see whether [Eliza] has an idea that I havnt put into her head or a word that I havnt put into her mouth" (767). Eliza's dependency reinforces his disdain: she tells him, "You know I cant go back to the gutter, as you call it, and that I have no real friends in the world but you and the Colonel" (779).

But Derrida argues that a *supplement* can also be an improvement upon the original. Even enemies of writing, including Rousseau and Plato, have found writing indispensable for expressing and disseminating their ideas. In his *Confessions*, Rousseau admitted that he preferred writing to speech as a mode of self-expression: "The part that I have taken of writing and hiding myself is precisely the one that suits me. If I were present, one would never know what I was worth." Similarly, Eliza cannot show her true worth until she hides her cockney origins beneath the artificiality of cultured speech. Only in "absence" can she truly be "present." Her mature and articulate speeches in Act V demonstrate that her "supplemental" relationship with Higgins is positive as well as negative. Evaluating her own accomplishments, she tells him: "You cant take away the knowledge you gave me. You said I had a finer ear than you. And I can be civil and kind to people, which is more than you can" (780).

A more conventional playwright than Shaw might have been satisfied to pit Eliza and Higgins against each other in this way throughout the play. But Shaw, interested in the ambiguities of their relationship, makes Eliza herself ambivalent about her "supplemental" status. Having jettisoned her Lisson Grove identity, she feels like an exile. As she tells Higgins, "I am a child in your country" (770). We get a glimpse of her inner emptiness when she wistfully says, "I only want to be natural" (778). That heartfelt wish can never be granted, for Eliza—with no past and no peers—will never again feel the naturalness and belonging that Higgins finds among the moneyed classes. His is the favored position, for he is the source rather than the *supplement* in their relationship.

But Shaw, still exploring ambiguities, placed negatives as well as positives on Higgins's side. In a reversal of Platonic values, "presence" is a disadvantage to Higgins, for his habitual mode of self-expression is inferior to Eliza's artificial speech: "You damned impudent slut, you!" he shouts in one of the last speeches of the play (781). Even worse, Higgins believes himself incapable of improvement. His language habits are not much different from Eliza's Lisson Grove speech, as she observes: "I was brought up to be just like him, unable to control myself, and using bad language on the slightest provocation" (768). But while Eliza undergoes a powerful transformation, Higgins stubbornly clings to his Platonic belief in unalterable essences: "I cant change my nature; and I dont intend to change my manners" (773). He had freed Eliza from the prison of her former existence, but he refuses to do the same for himself.

—Jean Reynolds, "Deconstructing Henry Higgins, or Eliza as Derridean 'Text,'" in SHAW: The Annual of Bernard Shaw Studies, Volume 14, ed. Bernard F. Dukore (University Park, PA: Pennsylvania State University Press, 1994): pp. 211–212.

LOUIS CROMPTON ON ELIZA, CLARA, AND CLASS ANTAGONISMS

[A professor of English at the University of Nebraska, Louis Crompton is the author of *Byron and Greek Love: Homophobia In 19th Century England.* In this excerpt, Crompton concentrates on the opening of *Pygmalion* to show how Shaw's work emphasizes a difference not only in speech patterns but also in manners.]

It must be admitted at the start, however, that Shaw's preface is a somewhat misleading guide to the meaning of the play. There Shaw enthusiastically applauds the new scientific approach to language by phoneticians, if only because it raised pronunciation above the intense self-consciousness and class snobbery which had always bedeviled the subject in England. Then he goes on to imply that the main theme of his comedy will be phonetics. But it takes only a little reflection to realize that dialects, in and of themselves, have no intrinsic dramatic or social significance. Our response to them as pure sounds is largely arbitrary: a Brooklynite's pronunciation of "girl" may strike one ear as exquisitely refined (it did Shaw's) and another as comically vulgar. The real basis for our reaction to anyone's dialect is our association of particular kinds of speech with particular classes and particular manners. Here we are much closer to the real stuff of drama, and especially of comedy. Manners have been a central concern of the comic stage from Roman times through Shakespeare and Molière down to our own day. And, for all the shop talk about phonology, it is possible with a little analysis to see that it is really manners and not speech patterns that provide the clue to the character contrasts in *Pygmalion*, accents being, so to speak, merely their outer clothing.

Shaw's opening scene is admirably suited to bring out these contrasts. It is a brilliant little genre-piece that sets a group of proletarians—some timidly deferential, some sarcastically impolite—over against an impoverished middle-class family with genteel pretensions, a wealthy Anglo-Indian, and the haughtily self-sufficient Professor Higgins, all jostling beneath a church portico. The moment is chosen to show class antagonisms and personal idiosyncrasies at their sharpest. Brute necessity prompts a flower girl to wheedle a few last coins from the opera-goers while they in turn face that acid test of middle-class manners, the scramble for taxis in a sudden squall. The scene highlights two kinds of vulgarity. The first is the comico-pathetic, specifically lower-class vulgarity of the flower girl. Eliza is vulgarly familiar when she tries to coax money out of prospective customers, and vulgarly hysterical when she thinks she is suspected of soliciting as a prostitute, on the theory that, as she belongs to a class that cannot afford lawyers, she had best be loud and vigorous in her prostestations of virtue. Later, she is vulgarly keen on lording it—or ladying it—it over her neighbors with her windfall of coins. What is interesting, however, is that Shaw by no means regards vulgarity as specifically a class trait. All the time he is treating us to Eliza's plangent diphthongs he is also dissecting the manners of the girl in the middle-class family, Clara Eynsford Hill. Compared to Eliza, Clara comes off the worse. For Clara is also pushing, and, in her dealings with strangers, as vulgarly suspicious and as quick to take offense as the flower girl, her rebuke to Higgins—"Dont dare speak to me"—being less comically naïve than Eliza's "I'm a good girl, I am"—but just as silly. And Eliza's pushiness at least has the excuse of springing from her wholly understandable desire to escape from the squalor of the slums into a bourgeois world which can offer her some kind of independence and self-respect.

—Louis Crompton, *Shaw the Dramatist* (Lincoln: University of Nebraska Press, 1969): pp. 141–143.

BERNARD DUKORE ON THE FILM VERSION OF *PYGMALION*

[Bernard Dukore, a professor of theater at Hunter College in New York, has written extensively on Shaw. In this essay, Dukore examines the ending of the film version of *Pygmalion*, concluding that Shaw's vision was not followed for the movie. Dukore contends that Shaw clearly wanted no emphasis on a romantic denouement to his play.]

"I absolutely forbid . . . any suggestion that the middleaged bully and the girl of eighteen are lovers," Shaw cabled the Minneapolis Civic Theatre in 1948 when they requested permission to modify the ending of *Pygmalion*. In the proposed interpretation that provoked this unambiguous command, Minneapolis was at one with London. To Herbert Berebohm Tree, who under Shaw's direction played Henry Higgins in the play's premier in 1914, "it seemed natural and inevitable," as Richard Huggett explains, "that if a play had a hero, he should love and eventually marry the heroine of it." Shaw vetoed Tree's suggestion that following Eliza's departure in Act V he go to the balcony, throw flowers to her, and blow kisses her way. After the play opened, however, Shaw escaped to Yorkshire to recuperate from the strain of rehearsals with Tree and Mrs. Patrick Campbell (Eliza). With Shaw away, Tree seized the opportunity to sentimentalize the ending. When the unsuspecting author returned and saw the flowers-and-kisses business, he was naturally furious. In a famous but probably apocryphal exchange between star actor and playwright, Tree declared that since his ending made money Shaw ought to be grateful, and Shaw replied that since that ending made nonsense Tree ought to be shot.

Why, then, did Shaw subtitle *Pygmalion* "A Romance in Five Acts"? His answer: "I call it a romance because it is the story of a poor girl who meets a gentleman at a church door, and is transformed by him, like Cinderella, into a beautiful lady. That is what I call a romance. It is also what everybody else calls a romance; so we are all agreed for once." Leaving aside the question of whether "everybody else" defines "romance" in this manner, it is certainly clear what Shaw means by the term.

In 1938, about a quarter of a century after the London premiere of *Pygmalion*, an English movie version was made, with Leslie Howard as Higgins and Wendy Hiller as Eliza. Shaw wrote the screenplay, for which he received an Academy Award. The cast included Viola Tree, Herbert's daughter, in a bit role in the ballroom scene (one of several new scenes written specifically for the film), and David Tree, Viola's son and Herbert's grandson, as Freddy.

From the start, the movie version moved in the direction of Beerbohm Tree's interpretation of the end. As Donald P. Costello indicates, "Shaw was suspicious of [Leslie] Howard's screen image as a romantic idol. 'The public will like him and probably want him to marry Eliza,' said Shaw, 'which is just what I don't want.' Shaw wanted, instead, a determined antiromantic in the role. . . . " The playwright's particular choice was Charles Laughton. But Shaw lost. Howard played Higgins and, with Anthony Asquith, codirected the film. Octogenarian Shaw visited Pinewood Studios to celebrate the start of the filming, but apart from that visit he was not present at the making of *Pygmalion*. As Beerbohn Tree did when Shaw left town, the film's directorial duo, Asquith and Howard, with either the assistance or abetting silence of the producer (Gabriel Pascal, to whom Shaw entrusted his work), seized the opportunity to sentimentalize the ending. Theoretically, Shaw had the right to approve the final shooting script, but

Costello's assertion to the contrary notwithstanding, I have seen no evidence that he actually did.

—Bernard F. Dukore, "'The Middleaged Bully and the Girl of Eighteen': The Ending They *Didn't* Film," *The Shaw Review* 14, no. 3 (September 1971): pp. 102–103.

⊛

MARGERY M. MORGAN ON SHAW AND THE SOCIAL SYSTEM

[Margery M. Morgan of the University of Lancaster is the author of *The Shavian Playground*, which considers Shaw's treatment of feminist issues in relation to the events and other dramatic works of his day. In this excerpt, Morgan suggests that Shaw's focus was on the class system more than on the feminist movement.]

Pygmalion examines the assumptions of social superiority and inferiority that underlie the class system, and demonstrates how unconsciously regulated patterns of social behavior (etiquette opposed to more spontaneous manners) help preserve class distinctions. There is good reason to believe that Shaw had read Thorstein Veblen's *Theory of the Leisure Class*. In particular, this play is concerned with speech differences as hallmarks of class: a professor of phonetics sets up an experiment to prove that he can turn a slum girl into a lady by changing her speech habits, and the comic climax of this scheme—negative proof of the theory—is reached when the elegantly dressed Eliza, in the most ladylike of tones, uses the taboo expression, 'Not bloody likely!' in the drawing room. The play gains symmetry, and its argument is made more complex, through the introduction of a second scheme, whereby her father is elevated socially and transformed in character by a bequest of money. The schematic element is cut across by a conflict more genuinely desperate than in *The Doctor's Dilemma:* the struggle of the girl to liberate herself from the insensitive tyranny of the professor, who is himself determined to remain comfortably dominant. As in so many of his plays, Shaw guides audience response to *Pygmalion* by combining in it echoes of older legends that arouse particular, sometimes discordant, expectations and emotions. Here he links the Cinderella story, the classic of wish-fulfillment transformation from rags to riches in a conventionally hierarchical society, with variations on the Faust legend of the man who assumes forbidden superhuman powers: Frankenstein who creates a monstrous form of life (a more sinister analogue of the classical Pygmalion, the misogynist sculptor whose statue is brought to life in answer to his prayers), or Svengali (among the most successful recent roles of Beerbohn Tree, the first English actor to play Professor Higgins) who turns a young girl into a world-renowned singer by the arts of hypnotic possession. In every production of the play, the lure of the Cinderella plot is so strong, and Shaw's increasing self-protection as Higgins becomes so enticing, that the theme of the degradation of women and wastage of life in patriarchal society is all but submerged, even though it is spelt out in the dialogue.

The ambivalence of Shaw's attitude to the pre-war feminist movement is revealed in a group of plays worth considering alongside *Pygmalion*. *Fanny's First Play*, as it was produced at the Little Theatre in 1911, masquerades as the work of a suffragette—though the Induction and Epilogue written to sustain this pretence soften any challenge with an avuncular playfulness, and divert attention to new, peripheral material through recognisable parodies of leading contemporary theatre critics. Inset is a play as 'pleasant' as *You Never Can Tell*, in which Shavian idiosyncrasy is subdued to produce a light comedy that could almost have been written by the popular A. W. Pinero and that includes a footman, really the younger brother of a Duke, who claims relationship with J. M. Barrie's Admirable Crichton and anticipates the Jeeves of P. G. Wodehouse. Feminist values are assumed in the characterisation of Margaret Knox, as in many of the energetic young women, impatient of convention, in Shaw's later drama; perhaps feminism is there, too, in the unabashed merriment of 'Darling Dora,' euphemistically described as a *fille de joie*, who turns that phrase into an imaginative reality. The explicit interlinked themes are a plea for youth's freedom to live experimentally and a commentary on the folly of class distinctions, but it is the old woman, Mrs. Knox, who is promoted to oracular authority, towards the end of the play: a minor echo of Mrs. George who, dignified by mayoral robes and fallen into a trance, carries *Getting Married* beyond the range of laws and statute books into more abstract pronouncements on human life.

—Margery M. Morgan, *Bernard Shaw II: 1907–1950* (Windsor, England: Profile Books, 1982): pp. 9–11.

[Bernard F. Dukore provides another perspective on eco-
nomics and the class system portrayed in *Pygmalion* in this
excerpt; he points out several instances of the use of money
in the work to suggest that money can supersede the differences imposed by the English classist society.]

Critical in establishing the play's social concerns is the first act, which
displays several social classes. Whereas the poorer people register different degrees of intimidation when Higgins confronts them (Liza, at
the furthest extreme, is so terrified she bursts into tears), the wealthy
Pickering is not at all troubled by the note taker. When Pickering tries
to console Liza by telling her she has a right to live where she pleases,
a more knowledgeable and realistic bystander sarcastically comments,
"Park Lane, for instance." The first act hints at the financial circumstances of the Eynsford Hills. Clara pinches pennies: she is opposed to
her mother paying Liza for the flowers Freddy knocked out of her
hands; she insists, since her mother ignores her opposition, that Liza
give her change for sixpence; and, when Liza reveals she only acciden-
tally called Freddy by his right name, she exclaims that the sixpence
has been thrown away. The Eynsford Hills's difficulty in getting a cab
symbolizes the economic straits and their problems in functioning on
a level of society accustomed to using cabs (this point is highlighted
by the attitude of Liza, to whom a cab is a treat).

As money is an important aspect of social classes in capitalist society, so is it a key element of every act of this play. Apart from
Clara's concern about the sixpence in the first act, Higgins explains
how he earns a fat living from phonetics: "This is an age of upstarts.
Men begin in Kentish Town with £80 a year, and end in Park Lane
with a hundred thousand. They want to drop Kentish Town; but
they give themselves away every time they open their mouth." For a
fee, he teaches them how to avoid giving themselves away. Liza sells
flowers and obtains money (by begging as well as by selling) from
Mrs. Eynsford Hill, Pickering, and Higgins. Whereas Liza sells in Act
I, she offers to buy in Act II. When she proposes to pay for speech
lessons, Higgins make financial calculations and computes on the
basis of the percentage of her income what the equivalent offer
would be from a millionaire. Mrs. Pearce tries to persuade Higgins
to discuss wages for Liza, but he offhandedly instructs her to pay
Liza whatever is necessary and then impatiently adds that if she is

given money she will only spend it on drink. When Doolittle arrives in order to exploit his daughter, Higgins gives him five pounds in what Higgins later refers to as the sale of Liza. In the third act, Liza expresses her belief that someone killed her aunt in order to steal her straw hat and would have done so for the hat pin alone. Mrs. Eynsford Hill confesses to Mrs. Higgins that she and her children are poor. In Act IV, Higgins remarks that Pickering, who has lost the bet, will have to pay him an amount that "will make a big hole in two hundred pounds." When Higgins mentions that Liza might marry, Liza identifies the economic basis of that suggestion: "We were above that at the corner of Tottenham Court Road. . . . I sold flowers. I didnt sell myself. Now youve made a lady of me I'm not fit to sell anything else." She inquires whether her clothes and jewelry belong to her, for she does not wish to be accused of stealing anything. Act V reveals Doolittle's new income, the result of an inheritance. Whereas formerly he sponged off others, now, he complains, others will sponge off him. Whereas in Act II he made money from Liza, in Act V he is in a position to support her, as Mrs. Higgins expects he will. Higgins offers to adopt Liza as his daughter and to settle money on her, but Liza decides to earn a living and with her income to support Freddy.

The basic thrust of the parable is carried by the plot and situations. When Higgins explains—within earshot of Liza—the transformation of upstarts from eighty to a hundred thousand pounds a year and his ability to remove linguistic indications of their lower-class origins, he suggest the parable's basic social theme, the removal of class differences: that social classes do not represent a permanent condition, that one can change one's social class, and that characteristics of different social classes can be eliminated. Stated simply, the main plot centers upon Higgins thrusting Liza from one social class into another. His efforts, as he later tells his mother, consist of changing one human being "into quite a different human being by creating a new speech for her. It's filling up the deepest gulf that separates class from class and soul from soul." Liza recognizes this truth. She comes to Higgins so that he may transform her, by teaching her to "talk more genteel," from a street flower girl into a "lady in a flower shop." Though by changing her speech, manners, and habits (including cleanliness), Higgins removes her from her social class, he ignores the question of how she is to earn her living afterwards, for he pushes her not one but several rungs up the class ladder. He makes her a lady rather than a shopgirl. It is Liza herself who accomplishes the next social transformation: from a lady, who does not and cannot earn her income, to a member of a professional class, like Higgins himself, and like Higgins she hopes to earn a living by teaching phonetics.

—Bernard F. Dukore, *Bernard Shaw, Playwright: Aspects of Shavian Drama* (Columbia: University of Missouri Press, 1973): pp. 286–288.

Plot Summary of
Saint Joan

The play contains six scenes or acts, followed by an epilogue that continues the story of Joan after her execution. Shaw also provided an expansive **Preface** to the play in which he explains the legend of Joan and gives his version of the history of the Church and its treatment of heretics in the Middle Ages.

The play's six scenes take Joan through her rise from an unknown peasant girl to the leader of the French armies during the Hundred Years' War. Each of the first three scenes is a dialogue between Joan and a doubter, and the climax of each occurs when a miracle convinces the doubter. These first scenes follow the same pattern: Joan's entrance, dialogue, and conquest.

The play opens, in **Scene I,** in the spring of 1429 in the castle of Vaucouleurs near Lorraine. An unsympathetic and demanding Robert de Baudricourt scolds and mistreats his steward because there are no eggs or milk. The steward's unlikely explanation is that the Maid of Lorraine, as Saint Joan is called, has made the hens stop laying and the cows stop giving milk. He explains that all have been bewitched and will continue that way as long as Joan remains waiting, unattended and ignored by Baudricourt, outside the castle. The steward also recounts that Joan has made use of her time while waiting by talking to the soldiers and gaining their confidence. Baudricourt finally relents and summons Joan into the castle. She greets him by ordering him:

> JOAN: . . . Captain: you are to give me a horse and armor and some soldiers, and send me to the Dauphin. Those are your orders from my Lord.
> ROBERT: Orders from your lord! And who the devil may your lord be? Go back to him, and tell him that I am neither duke nor peer at his orders: I am squire of Baudricourt; and I take no orders except from the king.
> JOAN: Yes, squire: that is all right. My Lord is the King of Heaven.

With this initial exchange, Baudricourt concludes that Joan is insane. Joan further explains that her Lord wants her to raise the siege of Orleans for the Dauphin, the uncrowned Charles VII. Baudricourt soon realizes, though, that the girl already has Bertrand de Poulengey and others on her side. He summons Poulengey to the castle. When they talk in private, Baudricourt, assuming that Poulengey is interested in Joan only because she is a woman, tries to dissuade Poulengey from any such liaison. But Poulengey convinces him that he feels no physical attraction to Joan, since he could think neither of the Blessed Virgin nor Joan in that way.

Although Poulengey does not know for sure if Joan can accomplish such high goals, he tells Baudricourt that there is no other way to aid the Dauphin. Poulengey offers to pay for Joan's horse and to accompany her. When Baudricourt calls Joan back into the room, he insists that she explain more about her orders from the Lord and how she receives them. While Joan does not want to discuss the voices she hears, she clearly demonstrates for Poulengey and Baudricourt that she is determined to crown the Dauphin at Rheims Cathedral and drive the English from France. She responds to Baudricourt's admonitions about the English by saying that she is not afraid of them, their English Black Prince, or the "goddams," as Baudricourt refers to the English soldiers. Joan continues by explaining why the French have yet to win:

> You do not understand, squire. Our soldiers are always beaten because they are fighting only to save their skins; and the shortest way to save your skin is to run away. Our knights are thinking only of the money they will make in ransoms: it is not kill or be killed with them, but pay or be paid. But I will teach them all to fight that the will of God may be done in France; and then they will drive the poor goddams before them like sheep.

As the scene ends, Baudricourt reluctantly tells Joan to go to Chinon to the Dauphin. As Joan and Poulengey leave, the steward bursts into the room to announce that the hens have begun to lay eggs again.

Scene II takes place at Chinon in Touraine in March of 1429. The Archbishop and the Lord Chamberlain, La Trémouille, are impatiently awaiting the arrival of the Dauphin. As they wait, they complain about him and his poor financial status. Gilles de Rais, Bluebeard, comes in to tell them that La Hire, a soldier hardened and with no manners, has been frightened mad. At this comment, La Hire bursts in to announce that a soldier has fallen to his death because he saw an angel. The three men are all shocked that La Hire would believe or even speak of such an event, when finally the Dauphin arrives.

The Archbishop and La Trémouille treat him harshly, despite the fact that he is their uncrowned king. As they continue to lecture him, the Dauphin interrupts to say that Robert de Baudricourt is sending him an angel. The Archbishop reveals that he knows of this plan and that the person is no angel, rather a country girl dressed as a soldier. As this comment, La Hire becomes unsettled again, because the girl is the same angel that caused the soldier to fall to his death.

All in attendance plan to test Joan when she arrives. Bluebeard agrees to pretend that he is the king and the Chamberlain's wife will stand in as the queen. But the Archbishop is sure that Joan will see through the ruse because it is well known that the Dauphin is unattractive and that Gilles has a blue beard. The Archbishop suggests Joan will ostensibly perform a miracle. Since he has more experience than they do with miracles, the Archbishop explains how Joan will do this:

> Parables are not lies because they describe events that have never happened. Miracles are not frauds because they are often—I do not say always—very simple and innocent contrivances by which the priest fortifies the faith of his flock. When this girl picks out the Dauphin among his courtiers, it will not be a miracle for me, because I shall know how it has been done, and my faith will not be increased. But as for the others, if they feel the thrill of the supernatural, and forget their sinful clay in a sudden sense of the glory of God, it will be a miracle and a blessed one. And you will find that the girl will be more affected than anyone else. She will forget how she really picked him out. So, perhaps, will you.

When Joan enters, she recognizes the real Dauphin immediately. She and the Archbishop exchange words causing laughter among the others, but the Archbishop remains serious with her.

Joan asks to speak with the Dauphin privately. When they are alone, the Dauphin confesses that he is afraid and tells Joan that the Archbishop and La Trémouille bully him. Joan asks him to concentrate on being a king: "I tell thee it is God's business we are here to do: not our own. I have a message to thee from God; and thou must listen to it, though thy heart break with the terror of it." Joan further announces:

> . . . And I come from God to tell thee to kneel in the cathedral and solemnly give thy kingdom to Him for ever and ever, and become the greatest king in the world as His steward and His bailiff, His soldier and His servant. The very clay of France will become holy: her soldiers will be the soldiers of God: the rebel dukes will be rebels against God: the English will fall on their knees and beg thee let them return to their lawful homes in peace.

The Dauphin agrees to the risk. He calls everyone back into the chamber. La Hire and the others kneel with Joan in prayer as the Archbishop gives them benediction and the scene ends.

The setting for **Scene III** is Orleans in April of 1429. Dunois, in charge of the French troops at the river and surrounded by the English, pays attention to the prevailing winds. He and his page see a kingfisher flying through the reeds near the river. They remark on the blue color of the bird in flight.

Joan enters. Dunois insists to her that his way of fighting the English is better because it is based on experience and wise counsel. But Joan maintains that the King of Heaven is on her side. She explains why her method is preferable since she is a soldier of God:

> I will never take a husband. A man in Toul took an action against me for breach of promise; but I never promised him. I am a soldier: I do not want to be thought of as a woman. I will not dress as a woman. I do not care for the things women care for. They dream of lovers, and of money. I dream of leading a charge, and of placing the big guns. You soldiers do not know how to use the big guns: you think you can win battles with a great noise and smoke.

With this and other zealous words, Joan convinces Dunois, who believes in her courage and desire to win. Nevertheless, Dunois insists on waiting for a change in the wind. The soldiers cannot cross the river in boats with the winds against them. He has prayed and lit candles to this end, but now Dunois asks that Joan light candles too. As Joan agrees, Dunois' page enters to tell his master that the winds have changed. They go off to battle, calling on God as the scene closes.

In the fourth scene, Shaw changes the pattern of action. Joan is absent from this scene, and Shaw uses one of his favorite devices: a discussion between equals. In a tent in the English camp the Earl of Warwick and the Chaplain de Stogumber discuss the English defeat at the hands of the French as **Scene IV** opens. Warwick pretends to be occupied by reading an illuminated Book of Hours. De Stogumber is unable to contain his anger at Joan and Dunois for their routing of the English. While Warwick reads, he tries to convince de Stogumber that patience is important, for all has not yet been lost. Warwick reveals the plan he has devised to bring about their revenge.

> THE NOBLEMAN: Easy, man, easy: we shall burn the witch and beat the bastard all in good time. Indeed I am waiting at present for the Bishop

of Beauvais, to arrange the burning with him. He has been turned out of his diocese by her faction.

THE CHAPLAIN: You have first to catch her, my lord.

THE NOBLEMAN: Or buy her. I will offer a king's ransom.

When Cauchon, the Bishop of Beauvais, arrives, both Englishmen treat him respectfully but quickly get to the point of having Joan burned. De Stogumber shows no subtlety in dealing with the subject; his comments betray his nationalistic feelings. Warwick, on the other hand, tries to deal with Cauchon more discreetly in order to bring him to Warwick's side. The elder Bishop is an experienced cleric and repeatedly stresses the differences between temporal and spiritual authorities:

CAUCHON: I cannot burn her. The Church cannot take life. And my first duty is to seek this girl's salvation.

WARWICK: No doubt. But you do burn people occasionally.

CAUCHON: No. When the Church cuts off an obstinate heretic as a dead branch from the tree of life, the heretic is handed over to the secular arm. The Church has no part in what the secular arm may see fit to do.

WARWICK: Precisely. And I shall be the secular arm in this case. Well, my lord, hand over your dead branch; and I will see that the fire is ready for it. If you will answer for the Church's part, I will answer for the secular part.

The discussion continues. The Chaplain enrages the sensitivities of Cauchon, who finds it necessary to lecture both men on the devil and the Church. But he concludes that if Joan does not recant her sin of heresy, "to the fire she shall go if she once falls into my hands."

Warwick, not content to leave the debate on a spiritual level, expands his assertions by claiming that Joan threatens the kings and secular world as well as the spiritual one. But Cauchon changes his tone of disagreement and suggests to Warwick that they should unite their energies:

CAUCHON: . . . I see now that what is in your mind is not that this girl has never once mentioned The Church, and thinks only of God and herself, but that she has never once mentioned the peerage, and thinks only of the king and herself.

WARWICK: Quite so. These two ideas of hers are the same idea at the bottom. It goes deep, my lord. It is the protest of the individual soul against the interference of priest or peer between the private man and his God. I should call it Protestantism if I had to find a name for it.

CAUCHON: . . . Scratch an Englishman, and find a Protestant. (pp. 98–9)

Echoing Shaw's thoughts, the Bishop and the Earl come to an unofficially declared agreement on Joan's fate as the scene ends.

A beautifully dressed Joan prays in the Rheims cathedral as **Scene V** opens. Dunois enters and calls her to join the crowds that are celebrating the King's crowning outside. Joan confesses that she prefers the time before a battle instead of the reaction afterwards. She asks Dunois to explain why the noblemen and churchmen hate her. Dunois does not hesitate:

> Do you expect stupid people to love you for showing them up? Do blundering old military dug-outs love the successful young captains who supersede them? Do ambitious politicians love the climbers who take the front seats from them? Do archbishops enjoy being played off their own altars, even by saints? Why, I should be jealous of you myself if I were ambitious enough.

Dunois warns her not to go too far by thinking of taking Paris. Joan, instead, explains that her voices give her the strength to go on.

King Charles, Bluebeard, and La Hire come into the cathedral vestry. There, Joan tells the King that her job is finished so she plans to return to the country. Joan notes that none of them will miss her. Worse still, she predicts that she shall only last a year. Nevertheless, Joan tries once more to convince Dunois to take Paris with her. Her zeal makes her even confront the Archbishop. To their taunting, Joan responds: "But I do know better than any of you seem to. And I am not proud: I never speak unless I know I am right." The discussion goes on; there is some more taunting but Dunois speaks on Joan's behalf. He touches a nerve, though, when he suggests that Joan's zeal will lead her eventually into the enemy's hands. Dunois challenges them: "And now tell me, all of you, which of you will lift a finger to save Joan once the English have got her?" The Archbishop follows up on Dunois's warning by explaining how Cauchon and the Church will proceed against her. He issues a last warning: "If you perish through setting your private judgment above the instructions of your spiritual directors, the Church disowns you, and leaves you to whatever fate your presumption may bring upon you. . . . You stand alone: absolutely alone. . . . " But Joan defies him yet again by responding: "I have better friends and better counsel than yours." As the scene closes, all have clearly abandoned her.

Scene VI opens in Rouen in May of 1431. Joan is about to be tried in Cauchon's court, with the Inquisition participating. Warwick and

Cauchon talk briefly at the opening of the scene and Warwick questions why the trial has not yet begun when they captured Joan over nine months earlier. The Bishop explains that the proceedings have only just reached his level, because an investigation has taken place in preparation for the trial. The Inquisitor and D'Estivet, the prosecutor, join them. The men exchange barbs about temporal authority interfering with spiritual matters. Courcelles interrupts them to complain to the Inquisitor. Courcelles is visibly upset that the 64 counts he has prepared against Joan have been reduced to 12. The Inquisitor tries to explain that only one count—that of heresy—is necessary to condemn her to burn. The young priest Ladvenu tries to intervene to suggest mercy. This gives the Inquisitor an opportunity to warn them on the evils of the heresies that he has seen in the fulfillment of his duties. The Inquisitor explains:

> [Y]ou must be on your guard against your natural compassion. You are all, I hope, merciful men: how else could you have devoted your lives to the service of our gentle Savior? You are going to see before you a young girl, pious and chaste. . . . The devilish pride that has led her into her present peril has left no mark on her countenance. . . . Therefore be on your guard.

When Joan appears, she wears chains around her ankles and she looks pale. She explains that the food she was given made her ill. Joan further recounts that the doctors sent to cure her would not bleed her "because the silly people believe that a witch's witchery leaves her if she is bled." The chains are a result of Joan's attempt to escape. She defies them again by asking "Am I a heretic because I try to escape from prison?"

The Inquisitor reminds everyone that the proceedings have officially begun. Courcelles asks if Joan is to be tortured. Cauchon intercedes and puts an end to the discussion of torture. Cauchon prefers, instead, to question Joan about her obedience to the Church. Joan attests that she will obey the Church, "provided it does not command anything impossible," such as commanding her to say that the voices she has heard were not from God. Joan debates with those in charge and remains firm in her belief that "God must be served first." They insist that Joan change her clothing to that more suitable for a woman.

The questioning goes on until the Executioner enters to say that the stake is ready. This visibly shocks Joan, who maintains that the voices have told her she would not be burned. Cauchon tries to turn her, and

Joan agrees to recant. Though she cannot write, she makes her mark on the document after Ladvenu reads the text of the confession to her. Once she signs, the Inquisitor happily frees her from excommunication but condemns her to life in prison on bread and water. At this news, Joan proclaims that her voices were right after all:

> Yes: they told me you were fools, and that I was not to listen to your fine words nor trust to your charity. You promised me my life; but you lied. You think that life is nothing but not being stone dead. . . . But to shut me from the light of the sky and the sight of the fields and flowers . . . and keep from me everything that brings me back to the love of God when your wickedness and foolishness tempt me to hate Him: all this is worse that the furnace in the Bible that was heated seven times.

At this reaction, the authorities are agreed. They declare Joan a relapsed heretic and turn her over to the secular powers for burning. Some react with fear, some try to avoid watching the execution. The scene ends with Warwick questioning the Executioner:

> WARWICK: . . . I have your word, have I, that nothing remains, not a bone, not a nail, not a hair?
> THE EXECUTIONER: Her heart would not burn, my lord; but everything that was left is at the bottom of the river. You have heard the last of her.
> WARWICK: The last of her? Hm! I wonder.

The **Epilogue** takes place in June of 1456 at one of the chateaux of King Charles VII. The priest, Brother Martin Ladvenu, visits the King to tell him that justice at last has been served. He informs Charles that the sentence against Joan has been annulled. Charles goes to sleep in his chamber after dispatching the priest. He talks with Joan in his dream. Charles tells her of the years after her execution. Then others from Joan's past join the dream. Cauchon, Dunois, de Stogumber, Warwick, the Archbishop, along with others, appear to recount their fates after her unjust trial and execution. Once again, each one abandons her and Charles falls back to sleep.

This epilogue was much criticized by viewers. They thought it unnecessary, unartistic, inappropriate. Shaw was determined to keep it as part of the play, however, for the Epilogue was the medium he needed to make the play into the kind of tragedy he wanted it to be. He wrote it after the Easter Rebellion of 1916, and the epilogue dramatizes the same sort of needless destruction and loss of life as was true of the rebellion. Joan's life and the Easter Rebellion were both tragedies because they were a waste of effort and life. ❂

List of Characters in
Saint Joan

Robert de Baudricourt is a squire who bullies his steward to cover up his own lack of gumption. Baudricourt is forced to confront the following of devotees that Joan has quickly acquired in his region. He prefers to think more in military terms than to accept issues of faith.

The **Steward** judges Joan's success by the local hen's laying of eggs.

Joan, the Maid from Domrémy, manages to win over all who come in contact with her by steadfastly stating that she is fulfilling her Lord's wishes. In the medieval system of the day, most listeners interpret this stance as disrespect, until Joan explains that she hears the words of the Lord her God, delivered to her by the voices of St. Margaret and St. Catherine. Joan wins the siege of Orleans, sees the Dauphin recognized as Charles VII, and despite her religious fervor manages to enrage all the spiritual and temporal leaders of the day.

Bertrand de Poulengey, one of Joan's early allies, helps convince Baudricourt to assist Joan.

A dignified, imposing but not overly religious cleric, the **Archbishop of Rheims** warns Joan early on that her fervor will be her undoing.

La Trémouille, Constable of France, is an arrogant and unschooled nobleman with an uncontrolled temper. La Trémouille strongly opposes Joan's plans to take Orleans.

An extravagant young man who dies his beard blue, **Gilles de Rais** tries to please without success. Bluebeard pretends to be the King so all present can test Joan's powers.

Much more military than courtly, **Captain La Hire** does not waste time in pleasantries. Joan's fighting zeal eventually convinces him.

The Dauphin (later Charles VII) is physically weak and quite unattractive. The uncrowned Dauphin is capable of defending himself by his wit but cowers under the relentless criticisms of others at court. Joan fulfills her promise to crown him King at Rheims.

A young yet experienced and capable soldier, **Dunois** deals with Joan as with another soldier. He delays the river crossing to attack the English until the wind changes, putting his faith in God and then in Joan. But as Joan's fate is compromised, Dunois will not risk himself or his army to save her.

Richard de Beauchamp, Earl of Warwick, is Joan's temporal foe. Compared to his clerical companion, de Stogumber, Warwick is coolly calculating and wishes to bring Cauchon to his side in a political conspiracy against Joan.

Enraged at the English defeat at Orleans, **Chaplain de Stogumber** encourages Warwick to avenge the English against Joan and the French. De Stogumber's outrage takes over in his dealings with Warwick and Cauchon. He is the least thoughtful and most set on vengeance.

Peter Cauchon is Bishop of Beauvais. An older man, Cauchon is shrewdly aware of the significance of Warwick's plot. But Cauchon attempts to make them all focus on Joan's heresy. Outwardly, Cauchon maintains that he wants Joan's salvation, but as her spiritual foe, he is convinced she will not survive a trial.

The Inquisitor is an elderly and patient cleric whose outside demeanor does not reveal his authority and moral steadfastness. The Inquisitor contends that Joan and her own works will condemn her without his intervention. The Inquisitor frequently explains the position of the Church and the actions of the Holy Office (The Inquisition).

D'Estivet, Joan's prosecutor in her trial-by-law (as opposed to a trial by jury), in the opinion of Cauchon and the Inquisitor, tends to speak too long and too eloquently.

Inspired perhaps by religious zeal, **Canon de Courcelles** insists on bringing 64 counts against Joan in the indictment against her. Most of these accusations are superfluous in the Inquisitor's opinion.

A young priest who prefers mercy to the exaggerated demands of Courcelles, **Brother Martin Ladvenu** tries to guide Joan to sign her confession. ❀

Critical Views on
Saint Joan

GEORGE BERNARD SHAW ON PRONUNCIATION IN THE PLAY

[Shaw responds to Ms. Helburn's position that the pronunciation of French words in the New York production of *Saint
Joan* not be changed, as Shaw had desired, to more anglicized
forms. Shaw's letter to her is brief and humorous but clearly
shows his direct involvement and control in the productions
of his works.]

To THERESA HELBURN

[10 Adelphi Terrace WC2]
21st march 1924

Terry, dear, you know but little of the world.
The population of New York City is 5,620,048. The odd 48 know
that the French call Rheims Rah'ce, and themselves call it variously
Rance, Ranks, Rangs, Wrongs, Rass or Rams. The other 5,620,000
wonder what the 48 are trying to say, and call it Reems.
The 48 also call the Dauphin the Dough-fang or the Doo-fong.
The public laughs, and writes to me about it.
The 48 call Agincourt (an English word unknown in France) Adj
Ann Coor.
You had better do what I tell you every time, because I am older than
you—at least my fancy pictures you younger, and very beautiful.

GBS

—George Bernard Shaw, Letter to Theresa Helburn, 21 March 1924, in
Bernard Shaw: Collected Letters 1911–1925, ed. Dan H. Laurence (New
York: Viking, 1985): pp. 872–873.

⊗

CHARLES A. BERST ON INFLUENCES ON THE PLAY

[Charles A. Berst, professor of English at UCLA and author of
Bernard Shaw and the Art of Drama, is also editor of *SHAW 1:*

Shaw and Religion. In this excerpt, Berst questions *Saint Joan's* suggested indebtedness to Eliot's *The Waste Land* and Frazer's *Golden Bough.* He favors instead earlier influences of miracle and morality plays.]

Similarities between *Saint Joan* and *The Waste Land* may thus reflect similar sources, not indebtedness. Stanley Weintraub suggests a source as remote in time from *Joan* as the poem was close to it, revealing, as others have for *The Waste Land,* how various the play's wellsprings are. He cites an 1886 art review in which Shaw critiqued a painting by Robert Browning's son Barrett, titled "Joan of Arc and the Kingfisher." Since the painting featured a nude, Shaw dismissed its title as "a humorous imposture," yet he also noted that Barrett had brought the standing figure "into startling relief against a background of vivid verdure." This image may have influenced his third scene, where Joan stands as a fertilizing force in stark relief against a similar river setting. The nude seems a far cry from the splendidly armored Maid of Scene 3, but her contrast with the background and her momentary action as she looks over her shoulder to catch sight of the kingfisher are highly theatrical.

More immediately presenting *Waste Land* motifs prior to the poem is Shaw's 1915 Preface to *Androcles and the Lion.* Here, Shaw cites the regeneration myths of Frazer's *Golden Bough* along with the peasant's song of John Barleycorn, in which "the same primitive logic" appears: "that God is in the seed, and that God is immortal. And thus it became the test of Godhead that nothing you could do to it could kill it, and that when you buried it, it would rise again in renewed life. . . . And from the interweaving of these two traditions with the craving for the Redeemer, you at last get the conviction that when the Redeemer comes he will be immortal. Prior to Weston, this links the myths to Christianity and reveals Shaw's sensitivity to "interweaving," "craving," and "conviction," qualities he orchestrated in *Joan.*

At the same time, Shaw's intimate knowledge of Wagner undoubtedly led him to anticipate Weston's relating of fertility myths to the Grail legend since the myths had converged nearly forty years before in *Parsifal's* wounded flagging king, frustrated impotent court, stainless questing knight, and regenerating Grail and lance. Early in the opera's third act, Parsifal thrusts the lance into the ground and kneels before it in a prayer of spiritual hope, prefiguring the lance in *Joan's* third scene, Dunois's invocation to the Virgin, and his desire that Joan accompany him to church for prayer. As Parsifal heals the Grail king and supersedes him, regenerating the grail knights for their holy cause, so Joan heals and spiritually transcends the Dauphin, regenerating his dispirited troops for a cause she finds holy. In contrast, *The Waste Land* features a want of healing, spirit, and transcendence.

Shaw's knowledge of Frazer and Wagner thus suggests that by the time Weston sparked the metaphoric crux of Eliot's *Waste Land*, the crux was old hat for him. Moreover, while *Saint Joan's* metaphors function much as do those of Hopkins, they also resemble Wagner's musical conveyance of action, characters, and themes. Both allegorically and thematically, for example, Joan embodies Regeneration; Charles, Impotence; Stogumber, Jingoism; Warwick, Aristocracy; Cauchon and the Inquisitor, the Church. Forwarded and enriched by such motifs, the first three scenes rise to a crescendo driven by Joan's triumphant spirit, the last three present a countermovement as institutional powers coalesce against her, and the Epilogue provides a coda that mixes the two.

Reflecting ancient Greek origins are the play's fateful progression, Joan's Promethian nature, her premonition that she will last but a year, her offstage martyrdom, the satyr-play quality of the Epilogue, and the issue of Joan's pride, set forth by the Archbishop: "The old Greek tragedy is rising among us. It is the chastisement of hubris" (6:146). Reflecting medieval origins, miracle play elements dominate the first three scenes, morality play characters representing institutions prevail in the last three, and mystery play elements climax with Joan's resurrection in the Epilogue.

> —Charles A. Berst, "As Kingfishers Catch Fire: The Saints and Poetics of Shaw and T. S. Eliot," in *SHAW: The Annual of Bernard Shaw Studies, Vol. 1*, ed. Bernard F. Dukore (University Park, PA: Pennsylvania State University Press, 1994): pp. 120–121.

☙

CHRISTOPHER HOLLIS ON HISTORICAL MISREPRESENTATION IN SAINT JOAN

[A journalist and the son of an Anglican bishop, Christopher Hollis (1902–1977) converted to Catholicism around the same time as the first London production of *Saint Joan*, in 1924. Hollis wrote histories on Saint Ignatius, Thomas More, and the converts Newman and Chesterton, as well as many essays on sainthood and Catholisicm. Here Hollis, in an excerpt from an article first published in *The Dublin Review* in April 1928, discusses the historical misrepresentations he sees in *Saint Joan*.]

We find, then, in an examination of Mr. Shaw's *St. Joan*, that it contains historical misrepresentations of three kinds. The first kind is small and need not detain us. Writing not as an historian but as a dramatist, Mr. Shaw has, of course, as must all dramatists, altered and concentrated the facts of history so as to give them more dramatic power. Thus, as he himself says in his Preface, the two characters of Dunois and the Duc d'Alençon are knocked into one, thereby saving the theatre manager a salary and a suit of armour. Rightly, too, St. Joan's trial, recantation, and burning are all concentrated into a single scene. Doubtless there are other instances. It would be a waste of time to search them out.

The other two kinds of historical misrepresentation are more worthy of notice. They are misrepresentations not only of the incidents but of the spirit of the story of St. Joan, and misrepresentations of the institutions which he criticizes.

Let us consider the first of these two kinds and let us begin with small things. In ascribing to him the invention of the word "Protestant" Mr. Shaw pays a large tribute to the Earl of Warwick's mastery of a phrase. That would matter very little if only he made the Earl of Warwick, when he invented the phrase, use it with the right meaning. He does not do so. He imagines, like the Irish nurse in Mr. Wells's *Meanwhile*, that "Protestants protest against Roman Catholics." Historically, at least, they do not. Catholics, if anybody, protest against Catholics, Protestants protest against the toleration of Catholics. It is with such a meaning that the word emerged, a century after the death of St. Joan, from the failure of the Diet of Worms, summoned to regulate the religious troubles of Germany in 1524.

Yet we do not want to sink into antiquarian pedantry. Let us rather consider the main purpose of Mr. Shaw's play.

The main purpose is to present a dramatic clash between the mediæval and the modern world. If that clash is to be dramatic, both worlds must be shown at their best. St. Joan's judges must be made to say everything that there is to be said for the medieval world; St. Joan to say everything that there is to be said for the modern. Such a formula demands a large violence to history. How conscious Mr. Shaw is of the violence which he is doing, it is not always easy to see.

—Christopher Hollis, "Mr. Shaw's *St. Joan*," in *SHAW: The Annual of Bernard Shaw Studies, Vol. 2,* ed. Stanley Weintraub (University Park, PA: Pennsylvania State University Press, 1982): pp. 158–159.

Judi Dench on Joan as a Rebel

[Judi Dench was an acclaimed British actress who played Joan in the 1966 Nottingham Playhouse production of *Saint Joan*. Holly Hill, a speech and theater professor, interviewed Dench and other notable actresses who played Joan for her essay "Saint Joan's Voices: Actresses on Shaw's Maid." In this extract, Dench comments on her perception of Joan as Saint.]

A lot that happens to Joan, I think, is luck. That may be a heinous thing to say, but in actual fact it is luck and drive. She was a catalyst, and that is as important as that maybe she was a saint. But it was a saint for somebody else to make up their minds about. Too many Joans make up their own minds that she's a saint from the moment she walks in. I don't think she is that. I think she's a rebel. Shaw himself was, you know, and I'm sure that Joan appealed to him because he saw something of himself in her—that immovability of somebody who thinks and knows they're right.

It is ignorance, I think, that makes part of Joan's mind so shut off—I mean not willing to see other people's points of view. And maybe that's also something to do with her youth, and the fact that she calls a spade a spade. I just remember that being the thread all the way through and certainly not playing in any way the saint. I mean, that very, very matter-of-fact bit about saying "I'll ask Saint Catherine and she'll send a west wind"—total assurance that she's on the level of the saints. That must have been intolerable for them.

I think I played Joan with a tremendous stubbornness and a dogged determination. I only pursued material, total belief, and under that canopy also came the saints and my belief that God had sent me and any belief that I had about what was right and what was wrong. I hope it wasn't monotonous in that way, but I can't talk about that—I don't know.

But I did want to cut across—in a way it's the same as Juliet behaving so badly sometimes. She behaves terribly irrationally and hysterically. It's the intolerance of youth that I played in Juliet for Zeffirelli in 1961—that terrible intolerance of simply lying on the ground with your hands over your ears and saying, "Don't speak to me about it." That is the doggedness that can also go out and win battles.

—Judi Dench in Holly Hill's "Saint Joan's Voices: Actresses on Shaw's Maid," in SHAW: The Annual of Bernard Shaw Studies, Vol. 6, ed. Stanley Weintraub (University Park, PA: Pennsylvania State University Press, 1986): pp. 145–146.

ROBERT COX ON JOAN AND JOHN THE BAPTIST

[Robert Cox is an English professor at Marshall University. In this excerpt, Cox discusses the similarities between Joan of Arc and John the Baptist, particularly in that they are both harbingers of a better world, while accused of working with the devil.]

Another Shaw heroic charcter fits well into the image of John the Baptist: Joan of Arc. In the preface to Saint Joan Shaw refers to the Maid as "the ambassador and plenipotentiary of God . . . a member of the Church Triumphant whilst still in flesh on earth" (17:3). Like John, Joan is the harbinger of a better world to come. John is credited with bridging the gap between Judaism and Christianity; Joan, although a devout Catholic, can be regarded as one of the first Protestant martyrs. Both John and Joan loudly cry the truth as they perceive it, and it is their refusal to recant their "heresies" that leads to their deaths. King Charles says of Joan, "If only she would keep quiet, or go home" (17:121), while John loses his head for his unwillingness to keep quiet about what he sees as incest practiced by the king (Matthew 14:3, Mark 6:17).

Joan was, like both John and Marchbanks, accused of consorting with the devil: Cauchon calls her "diabolically inspired . . . a witch and a heretic" (17:100), although it was not her "voices" that threatened the religious establishment. Rather, it was her naive failure to conform to existing conventions that condemned her, like John. The Inquisitor comments about such rebels: "All began as saintly simpletons . . . the woman who quarrels with her clothes, and puts on the dress of a man, is like the man who throws off his fur gown and dresses like John the Baptist: they are all followed . . . by bands of wild women and men . . . " (17:129–30).

Joan bypassed the intercessors of the Church; she claimed that her mission was directly ordained for her by God. John likewise was preordained for his mission; when his mother "Elizabeth heard the salutation of Mary, the babe leaped into her womb" (Luke 1:41). Similarly, Joan shared a preference for the Baptist's simple diet: "I can live on bread: when have I asked for more: It is no hardship to drink water if the water be clean. Bread has no sorrow for me, and water no affliction" (17:145). John's leadership qualities also compare favorably with Joan's. In the preface to *Saint Joan* Shaw describes her as "very capable: a born boss," and able to get people to do what she wanted them to do. The final and most striking comparison between John and Joan is the legend surrounding Joan as "the one who carried little children to be baptized of the water and the spirit" (17:16).

—Robert Cox, "John the Baptist: A Shavian Role Model," *The Independent Shavian* 24, no. 1 (1986): pp. 17–18.

⊗

WILLIAM SEARLE ON JOAN AS PROTESTANT

[Professor Searle, who taught English at the University of Pittsburgh when this article was published, presents the character of Joan as "Protestant" in the sense that she protests the authority of the Church in favor of God's will. In this selection, Searle examines Protestantism in Shaw's work as antiauthoritarianism.]

"Protestantism," then, has emerged historically as a "protest" against wrong-headed attempts to maintain authority by irrationalist methods. But it does not follow, Shaw maintains, that it is itself rationalistic. In response to one correspondent, who attempted to refute his claim that Joan was the first Protestant by pointing out that as early as the ninth century Johannes Scotus Erigena had opposed his own reason to the dogmatism of the Vatican, Shaw observed that Erigenist rationalism was not historic Protestantism, and that Joan's maxim "God must be served first," by which she sought to assert the superiority of her private judgement to the authority of the Church, was completely irrational.

Clearly this remark implies, not only that irrationalism is an inseparable feature of the Protestant mentality, but also that it is closely related to what Shaw regards as Protestant anti-authoritarianism. But the example of Erigena itself indicates just as clearly that one may rebel against authority without denying the sovereignty of reason; and in fact it is not by virtue of his anti-authoritarianism that the Protestant is an irrationalist. On the contrary, it is precisely his irrationalism that makes him anti-authoritarian; for, as the phrase "God must be served first" suggests, his reliance upon direct inspiration is bound to put him at odds with the "religion, law and order" of his time.

Hence from the very beginning Shaw conceived of his play as one which would show "the Church, the Inquisition, the Feudal System, with divine inspiration always beating against their too inelastic limits." And behind his interest in the subject, accordingly, lay his conviction that if anti-mystical rationalism which was dominating Western civilization in his own time were not to end by destroying that civilization altogether, it must be rescued by a prophet who was himself sufficiently inspired to succeed in returning his fellows to a sense of religious purpose. "We want a few mad people now," Shaw makes Poulengy remark in the first scene of *Saint Joan*. "See where the sane ones have landed us!" And when his friends the Hamons flubbed their French translation of that line, he warned them that it had been taken by readers and audiences as an allusion to the war of 1914–1918, and therefore had to close with more crispness than their "*ceux qui sont sains d'esprit.*"

By his own showing, then, Shaw, in choosing a "Protestant" as the subject for an heroic drama, was responding to what he took to be the urgent needs of the modern world. Yet in the very process of making this point he sometimes implies that the sort of rationalism with which Joan was forced to contend in the fifteenth century was very different from the atheistic materialism which her like would have to confront in the twentieth. Thus in the Preface he concluded a long attack against modern rationalism by declaring that "To Joan and her contemporaries we should appear as a drove of Gadarene swine, possessed by all the unclean spirits cast out by the faith and civilization of the Middle Ages, running violently down a steep place into a hell of high explosives."

From this it appears that modern rationalism differs from mediaeval in being fundamentally Godless; and in fact it is clear from a number of Shaw's remarks on the subject that he did not believe that rationalism need be materialistic. In the 1915 Preface to *Androcles and the Lion*, for instance, he describes Saint Paul himself as "an inveterate Roman Rationalist, always discarding the irrational real thing for the unreal but ratiocinable postulate." And the account of Paul's views which he makes in that work suggests that a rationalist in theology is one who, instead of turning directly to God for guidance, attempts to arrive at both his ethics and his metaphysics by theorizing about the implications of a given body of traditional doctrine.

So conceived, however, theological rationalism does in fact share one important feature in common with materialism: it represents, that is, an attempt to substitute the counsel of a dogmatic "reason" for that of inspiration in the conduct of the moral life. And to that extent it is very nearly as wrong-headed as materialism itself is, being rooted in an idealistic misconception of the reason which regards that faculty as transcendant and absolute and thus comes ultimately to identify it with God.

—William Searle, "Shaw's Saint Joan as 'Protestant,'" *The Shaw Review* 15, no. 3 (September 1972): pp. 111–112.

©

J. L. Wisenthal on the Anti-English Element in the Play

[J. L. Wisenthal is a professor of English at the University of British Columbia and the author of *The Marriage of Contraries: Bernard Shaw's Middle Plays* (1974) and *Shaw's Sense of History* (1988). In this excerpt from the former book, Wisenthal examines anti-English sentiment in *Saint Joan* and argues that Shaw easily found contemporary relevance in the historical character of Joan.]

No doubt one of the factors which attracted Shaw to Joan's history as a subject was the inevitable anti-English element in it. Joan's efforts were devoted to the expulsion of the English from France, and any reasonable presentation of her story would have to accept this as a legitimate and laudable aim. (*King Henry the Sixth, Part One*, it will be agreed, is not a reasonable presentation of her story.) The story by its nature is hostile to English imperialism, and in introducing this element into his play Shaw could not be accused of distortion. Again, Shaw saw the relevance of Joan's story to contemporary history. *Saint Joan* was begun just at the end of the civil war which followed the establishment of the Irish Free State in 1921, and part of it was written in Ireland. The parallel between early twentieth-century Ireland and early fifteenth-century France would have been in Shaw's mind: both France and Ireland were struggling for freedom from English domination, and the Irish case was based on the nationalism that Shaw ascribes to Joan in the play. The Preface (which stresses in various ways the contemporary relevance of Joan's trial and execution) compares the trial to that of Roger Casement in 1916 for treason against England, and Casement, like Joan, was executed by the English. In 1916 Shaw wrote a skillful defense for Casement himself to deliver at his trial; this speech, which Casement's lawyers did not make use of, was privately printed, with a prefatory note by Shaw, in 1922—the year before *Saint Joan* was begun.

One of the reasons why Shaw is able to combine historical veracity with his own world-view is that Joan herself, as she appears in the records of the trial, is such a Shavian sort of character. Several of her shorter speeches in the Trial Scene are taken almost verbatim from the records of what the actual Joan said to her judges. No historical character could have made a more appropriate subject for a dramatist who had created an impudent youth like Frank Gardner, an innocent and inspired youth like Marchbanks, a saintly, unconventional, and compelling young woman like Barbara Undershaft (to whom Joan is closest), and a Christian martyr (or near-martyr) like Lavinia. The prophetic character is one of Shaw's most common—and dramatically most successful—types, and he had for many years before writing *Saint Joan* wanted to write a play about Mahomet, who is compared to Joan both in the Preface and in the play (by Cauchon in the Tent Scene).

—J. L. Wisenthal, *The Marriage of Contraries: Bernard Shaw's Middle Plays* (Cambridge: Harvard University Press, 1974): pp. 173–174.

Works by
George Bernard Shaw

1885–92	*Widowers' Houses*
1893	*The Philanderer*
	Mrs. Warren's Profession
1894	*Arms and the Man*
	Candida
1895	*The Man of Destiny*
1895–97	*You Can Never Tell*
1897	*The Devil's Disciple*
1898	*Caesar and Cleopatra*
1899	*Captain Brassbound's Conversion*
1901	*The Admirable Bashville: or Constancy Unrewarded*
1901–3	*Man and Superman*
1904	*John Bull's Other Island*
	How He Lied to Her Husband
1905	*Major Barbara*
	Passion, Poison and Petrification
1906	*The Doctor's Dilemma*
1907	*The Interlude at the Playhouse*
1908	*Getting Married*
1909	*The Shewing-up of Blanco Posnet*
	Press Cuttings
	The Fascinating Foundling
	The Glimpse of Reality
1910	*Misalliance*
	The Dark Lady of the Sonnets
1911	*Fanny's First Play*
1912	*Androcles and the Lion*
	Overruled
	Pygmalion
1913	*Great Catherine*
1914	*The Music Cure*

1915	*O'Flaherty, V.C.*
1916	*Augustus does his Bit*
	The Inca of Perusalem
	Heartbreak House
1917	*Annajanska: The Bolshevik Empress*
1918–21	*Back to Methuselah*
1920	*Jitta's Atonement*
1923	*Saint Joan*
1929	*The Apple Cart*
1931	*Too True to be Good*
1933	*Village Wooing*
	On the Rocks
	The Six of Calais
1934	*The Simpleton of the Unexpected Isles*
1935–36	*The Millionairess*
1937	*Cymbeline Re-finished*
1938	*Geneva*
1939	*In Good King Charles' Golden Days*
1947	*Buoyant Billions*
1948	*Farfetched Fables*
1949	*Shakes versus Shav*
1950	*Why She Would Not* (unfinished)

Works about
George Bernard Shaw

Bentley, Eric. *Bernard Shaw.* New York: New Directions, 1957.

Berst, Charles A. *Bernard Shaw and the Art of Drama.* Urbana: University of Illinois Press, 1973.

Chesterton, G. K. *George Bernard Shaw.* New York: Folcroft Library Editions, 1978.

Costello, Donald P. *The Serpent's Eye: Shaw and the Cinema.* Notre Dame: University of Notre Dame Press, 1965.

Crane, Gladys M. "Shaw and Women's Lib." *The Shaw Review* 17(1974): 23–31.

Dervin, Daniel. *Bernard Shaw: A Psychological Study.* Lewisburg, PA: Bucknell University Press, 1975.

Dietrich, R. F. *Portrait of the Artist as a Young Superman: A Study of Shaw's Novels.* Gainesville: University of Florida Press, 1969.

Dunbar, Janet. *Mrs. G. B. S.: A Portrait.* New York: Harper and Row, 1963.

Dukore, Bernard F. *Bernard Shaw, Director.* Seattle: University of Washington Press, 1971.

———. "Revising *Major Barbara*." *The Shaw Review* 16 (1973): 2–10.

———. "The Time of *Major Barbara*." *Theatre Studies* 23 (1982): 110–111.

Gibbs, A. M., ed. *Shaw: Interviews and Recollections.* Iowa City: University of Iowa Press, 1990.

Holroyd, Michael. *Bernard Shaw.* 4 vols. New York, Random House, 1988, 1989, 1991, 1992.

Kaul, A. N. *The Action of English Comedy: Studies in the Encounter of Abstraction and Experience from Shakespeare to Shaw.* New Haven: Yale University Press, 1970.

Laurence, Dan H., ed. *Bernard Shaw: A Bibliography.* 2 vols. Oxford: Clarendon, 1983.

McInerney, John M. "'Shakespearean' Word-Music as a Dramatic Resource in Shaw." *The Shaw Review* 14–2 (May 1971): 90–94.

Meisel, Martin. *Shaw and the Nineteeth-Century Theatre*. Princeton: Princeton University Press, 1963.

Mencken, H.L. *George Bernard Shaw: His Plays*. Boston: John W. Luce, 1905.

Mills, John A. *Language and Laughter: Comic Diction in the Plays of Bernard Shaw*. Tucson: University of Arizona Press, 1969.

———. "Acting is Being: Bernard Shaw on the Art of the Actor." *The Shaw Review* 13–2 (May 1970): 65–78.

Morgan, Margery M. *The Shavian Playground: An Exploration of the Art of George Bernard Shaw*. London: Methuen, 1972.

Pease, Edward R. *The History of the Fabian Society*. New York: International Publishers, 1926.

Peters, Margot. *Shaw and the Actresses*. New York: Doubleday, 1980.

Peters, Sally. *Bernard Shaw: The Ascent of the Superman*. New Haven: Yale University Press, 1996.

Quinn, Martin. "The Informing Presence of Charles Dickens in Bernard Shaw's *Pygmalion*." *The Dickensian* 80–3 (Autumn 1984): 144–150.

Searle, William. *The Saint & the Skeptics: Joan of Arc in the Work of Mark Twain, Anatole France, and Bernard Shaw*. Detroit: Wayne State University Press, 1976.

The Shaw Review 20 (1977). Special Shaw issue.

Silver, Arnold. *Bernard Shaw: The Darker Side*. Stanford: Stanford University Press, 1982.

———. *Saint Joan: Playing with Fire*. New York: Twayne, 1993.

Ure, Peter. "Master and Pupil in Bernard Shaw." *Essays in Criticism* 19, no. 2 (April 1969): 118–139.

Watson, Barbara Bellow. *A Shavian Guide to the Intelligent Woman*. New York: W.W. Norton, 1972.

Weinreb, Ruth Plaut. "In Defense of Don Juan: Deceit and Hypocrisy in Tirso de Molina, Moliere, Mozart, and G. B. Shaw." *Romanic Review* 74–4 (November 1983): 425–440.

Weintraub, Rodelle, ed. *Fabian Feminist: Bernard Shaw and Women*. University Park: Pennsylvania State University Press, 1977.

Weintraub, Stanley. *Journey to Heartbreak: The Crucible Years of Bernard Shaw: 1914–1918*. New York: Weybright and Talley, 1971.

————, ed. *Shaw: An Autobiography: 1856–1898, 1898–1950*. 2 vols. New York: Weybright and Talley, 1969, 1970.

Weiss, Samuel A., editor. *Bernard Shaw's Letters to Siegfried Trebitsch*. Palo Alto: Stanford University Press, 1986.

Woodbridge, Homer E. *George Bernard Shaw: Creative Artist*. Carbondale: Southern Illinois University Press, 1963.

Index of
Themes and Ideas